The Politics of Consent

"wet" Tory

FRANCIS PYM

The Politics of Consent

HAMISH HAMILTON

LONDON

First published in Great Britain 1984
by Hamish Hamilton Ltd
Garden House, 57–59 Long Acre, London WC2E 9JZ

Copyright © 1984 by Francis Pym

ISBN 0-241-11351-2

Typeset by Rowland Phototypesetting Ltd, Bury St Edmunds, Suffolk
Printed and bound in Great Britain by
Billing & Sons Ltd, Worcester

Contents

Preface

I want to thank the friends who have helped me with this book. My principal counsellor and colleague throughout has been Jim Powell. I am especially grateful to him for his encouragement, his guidance and his enthusiasm.

Many others have helped too, either as specialists on a particular subject or as readers of the whole draft. They have each made invaluable comments and have saved me from many errors. My secretary, Penny Rankin, has performed miracles of typing at great speed – and without ever losing her cheerfulness.

I also owe much to my wife and family: they have all helped in different ways, and it is to them that I offer this book.

Everton, Bedfordshire
1 April 1984

Introduction

Whatever else may be said of it, my meeting with the Prime Minister on the evening of Friday, 10 June 1983 was brief and to the point. "Francis," she said, "I want a new Foreign Secretary."

Every problem is its own oppportunity. Despite my disagreement with some aspects of Government policy and approach, I was happy to remain in the Cabinet and to fight for my cause there. Breadth of opinion is vital to a good Government. However, my departure from office has given me the opportunity to recharge my batteries, to stand aside from the maelstrom of day-to-day events and to take a considered look at the country's problems and how they can be tackled.

This book is the first product of that opportunity. It gives a full account of my opinions on the main issues of the day: what I do believe, as well as what I do not. I have always tried to make a positive contribution to political debate and this remains my purpose. I have never criticised for the sake of it, but always with the intention of helping to improve the quality of government. I like to think I have received criticisms of myself in the same spirit. I welcome this type of criticism; what I do not welcome is the increasing habit of attacking anyone who expresses an independent point of view. Unanimity is deadening. A lively and constructive debate is not only healthy, it is the best way of reaching the right decisions – why assume that anyone knows all the answers? That is the first reason for writing the book.

There is also a second reason. I believe in a particular approach to politics which is variously described as 'the Disraelian tradition' or 'One Nation Conservatism'. This approach has characterised the party at its greatest moments and has ensured its survival as a broad party of government rather than as a narrow and dogmatic faction. The first quality of this tradition is to welcome and then to synthesise a wide spectrum of opinion. It is founded on the need to listen to people, whether one agrees with them or not. It demands a constant attempt to win their consent. It believes in building on the things that unite people and not exaggerating the things that divide them. It has become quite unfashionable.

People might ask, then, why I should write a book that some people will see as divisive. The literal, if pedantic, reply is that synthesis is formed from thesis and antithesis. When only the thesis is allowed to exist, as at present, unless one wholly accepts it, one is forced to take responsibility for the antithesis. Different views will always exist. Provided they are argued constructively, they need not be divisive. In my opinion, the origin of divisiveness is a refusal to accept the legitimacy of alternative views and a reluctance to tolerate their expression. At the moment, the only options for a Conservative Member of Parliament are to be praised as an echo, to be castigated as a rebel, or to say nothing. That is what I dislike about the current state of affairs. It promotes narrow-mindedness and intolerance. It adopts the principle that to veer even one degree off the true course is to miss the harbour. It ignores the fact that the coast is graced by many harbours, none of them perfect.

But fashions change. In time, the discarded notion that other people might have a valid point of view will re-emerge. In the meantime, my concern is that the flag of traditional Conservatism is kept flying, and that people are reminded of its values and its worth, so that one day a standard-bearer can pick it up and put it back at the centre of our affairs, where it belongs.

The values of this tradition are as much to do with the approach to politics as with specific policies. Although the book deals with both, its emphasis is on the approach. No amount of idealism and commitment can obscure the fact that politics concern decision-making and action. The politics of consent confront that fact: they are based on the proposition that it is both more attractive and more effective if Governments attempt to win the consent of the nation as a whole, rather than railroad people into partisan decisions. In that way, the policies are more acceptable at the time and are less likely to be reversed later.

Such an approach calls for an understanding of people and of circumstances. It calls for a harmony between individual ambition and wider social considerations. It calls for a recognition that we are all interdependent. It calls for tolerance and humour. It calls

for leadership that responds to people in the present and anticipates their needs in the future. It precludes dogma, ideology,
inflexibility, shortsightedness and intolerance. It asserts that life
itself is a balance and that politics must reflect this fact. That is
why my main political concern, now and always, is not to be the
permanent protagonist of a fixed point of view, but to make a
positive effort to redress whatever imbalance currently exists.

That is what I have tried to do in this book. Every chapter is
separate, but each derives from the same perspective and the
same approach. I hope it will be regarded as a constructive and
forward-looking contribution to political debate. Opinions are
the stuff of politics. They are not to be feared. The worst one can
envisage of someone else's opinions is that they might be right.

ONE

Mrs Thatcher's Government

'We often refuse to accept an idea merely because the tone of voice
in which it has been expressed is unsympathetic to us.'
– NIETZSCHE

'Margaret Thatcher is courageous and resolute. She speaks for
the people of Britain and is the first Prime Minister for decades to
have the guts to do what is necessary to put the country back on its
feet. She sticks up for the individual. She speaks for the moral
values we have lost. She has put pride and purpose back into the
nation. Francis Pym is ineffective and negative. He epitomises the
willingness to compromise that has led Britain downhill. He has
no practical alternatives to offer. All he does is whine about things
he does not have the nerve to do himself.'

'Margaret Thatcher is a dangerous, doctrinaire demagogue.
She has brought industrial disaster to the country because of an
inflexible refusal to adjust her bogus ideology. She is determined
to destroy the social services and to bring misery to working
people. Francis Pym had the courage to stand up to this tyranny
and look where it got him. He stands for the decent, compassion-
ate side of Conservatism. He is a man of principle and integrity.'

Neither paragraph is a direct quotation, yet the flavour of each
will seem familiar to anyone who reads the newspapers – especially the first, since it reflects the view of most Fleet Street prop-
rietors. The public is presented with one of these stereotypes and
told to agree with it. Failure to agree with the stated view, it is
suggested, means acceptance of the opposite view, and look how
ridiculous that is. No point in-between is on offer.

Of all the arguments advanced in this book, the one I most want
to communicate is that the habit of viewing life, politics and
personalities in black and white terms is both false and dangerous.
To reduce the complexities of life to two polarised contradictions
on every issue is to contradict the nature of life itself. Anyone who
approaches this book expecting either to agree or to disagree with

everything it says will, I hope, be disappointed. We may need to
simplify life in order to deal with it, but we should never assume
that life is simple, that any one person's conclusions are the truth
or that no alternatives exist.

Yet the spirit of the age encourages us to be absolutist.
Margaret Thatcher is in tune with this spirit and has perhaps
done more than anyone to create it. She likes everything to be
clear-cut: absolutely in favour of one thing, absolutely against
another. It is the opposite of my approach, which is no less
decisive, but which is to say – yes, we should take this action, but
we should do it in a particular way, because we must take into
account the legitimate view of this group or that. It is a mode of
thought that she dislikes: she prefers to go straight for her target.

Such an approach does not lack all merit: sometimes it is right
and necessary and the only way to get things done. But it is not my
preferred approach and not my style. I do not accept that
proposed courses of action are totally good or totally bad. I do not
accept that people are wholly right or wholly wrong. I do not
accept that one set of policies will lead to unalloyed triumph, nor
the other to unmitigated disaster. Yet this Government, more
than most, presents itself in such a way and most newspapers echo
the polarity. To be loyal means one hundred per cent acceptance
of Government thinking: any dissent, or even the admittance of
doubt, is treachery and treason. After nine years as party leader
and five as Prime Minister, Margaret Thatcher still asks people
the question, 'Are you one of us?', by which she means, 'Are you
completely free of any doubt as to the utter rightness of everything
we are doing?'

It will come as no surprise that I am not 'one of us'. I regard the
viewpoints expressed in the opening paragraphs as caricatures.
Both contain elements of the truth, but exaggerated to the point
where they become untrue. Truth must involve balance, which
both statements lack. Balance is tiresome. It means that one has to
think about things, to see other points of view, to abandon the
comforting crutch of certainty. How much simpler it is to declare
one's own convictions to be the truth and to have done with all the
difficulties. It is easy to fall victim to this process. Many people
must think that, since I am not an unqualified admirer of the
Government, I am its out and out critic. I am not. I admire a great

deal about both the Prime Minister and the Government, but not everything. So I would ask the reader to give up all pre-conceptions at this point, to approach the book in a spirit of balanced enquiry and to acknowledge that the rich colours of life cannot be reduced to black and white.

The second point I want to make at the outset also concerns balance. I believe that every positive characteristic has an opposite dimension and that the two are intrinsically related. If everything that I most dislike about the Government's approach was to be eradicated, much of what I most admire might well be eradicated also. The same is true of everyone and everything. The two sides of the coin may not be of equal value, but both sides exist. If one recognises this fact, one can find ways to obviate the weaknesses and enhance the strengths. In politics, I believe this argues the need for a Government – or any other group – which contains a range of complementary talents, rather than one with such similar talents that its collective weaknesses restrict its collective strengths. This belief, together with my sense of the overall balance of life, precludes me from seeing anything or anyone in wholly black and white terms. These attitudes colour the rest of the book.

I am too close to events to give an objective account of the Government's record since 1979 or of the Prime Minister's leadership. I do not present the assessment that follows as the truth, but as my perception of it. The story begins more than a decade ago. The starting point is to describe how a woman who was largely unknown and relatively inexperienced in government was able to topple a former Prime Minister as leader of the Conservative Party. In some ways, that remains the most out-standing of Margaret Thatcher's achievements.

At the end of 1973, Ted Heath was Prime Minister, enjoying the loyalty and support of the Conservative Party. His Govern-ment, of which Margaret Thatcher and I were both members, had encountered considerable problems, had made some political mistakes and was starting to provoke doubts amongst its suppor-ters. But there was no challenge to the leadership, no sign that one would develop, and every indication that the Government stood a reasonable chance of re-election in late 1974 or early 1975.

Little more than twelve months later, Ted Heath had lost two

elections, the confidence of the party and finally its leadership. All
this resulted from two substantial errors. The first was to call an
election in February 1974 on the issue of the miners' strike. At
that time, the Government had a workable majority, its position
on the strike was supported by most of the country and Parliament
had eighteen months of its term to run. Many people saw the
election either as opportunism, or as divisiveness, or as an
indication that the Government lacked confidence in its ability to
govern. They certainly thought it was unnecessary and expressed
their feelings accordingly. The narrowness of the result made
another election inevitable and, in my opinion, made another
Conservative defeat inevitable. That is when the second error was
made. Ted Heath showed no understanding of the fact that the
events of 1974 had called his leadership into question.

I considered both these judgments to be mistakes and said so to
Ted Heath on several occasions at the time. In January 1974 I told
him that I did not think the British people would understand him
if he called an election. Similarly, after the October election, I was
one of those who urged him to go voluntarily to the 1922
Committee, to justify his actions and to offer himself for re-
election as leader of the party. He did not do so immediately, and
by early 1975 an enforced leadership election became inevitable,
as did the fact that he would lose it. I like Ted Heath. I think he
was a good Prime Minister. I have a great deal of sympathy for his
political and economic outlook. But I think he lost the leadership
for reasons that were entirely of his own making and that it is truer
to say that he forfeited his claim to the loyalty of the Parliamentary
Party than that he was betrayed. I supported him in the leadership
election, but I can well understand why others did not.

Not only did Ted Heath's attitude ensure that he would lose
the leadership, but it also made it likely that his successor would
be someone very different. All the front-runners, Willie Whitelaw
especially, were loyal to Ted Heath and found it impossible to
stand against him on the first ballot. This meant that those who
did stand would not be 'Heathites' and that someone would have
the opportunity to establish a strong enough position to withstand
the entry of the 'Heathites' on the second ballot. This is exactly
what happened.

But Margaret Thatcher's victory was by no means a negative

one, even if it owed much to chance. Then as now, she exuded confidence and clarity more than any other candidate. Amidst the shambles and the doubts of that time, here was one person who could articulate a point of view with conviction. This was notable, not only because she was relatively junior, but also because until the last moment there was uncertainty as to who would carry the flag for the viewpoint then associated with Keith Joseph. She was a last-minute candidate, but still had the greatest poise and self-assurance. More than that, the views she expressed found an emotional echo in the party and subsequently in the country. She offered something different. People felt that on a range of issues there had been too many compromises that had turned out for the worst. They felt that our economic and industrial problems were so deep-rooted that middle-of-the-road policies could not solve them, and that something more radical and determined was required.

My judgment is that Margaret Thatcher became leader for three reasons: because she offered an approach that was new and in tune with the party's instincts at that time, because she articulated that approach with clarity and conviction, and because the circumstances of the election gave her a head start over both the incumbent and the main front-runners. The fact that she was a woman never came into it, which is both as it should be and a great tribute to her.

After her election, Margaret Thatcher was fortunate to have four years to prepare the ground for government. That time was needed and she used it very well. She was an excellent Opposition leader and I would not be surprised if she still felt those four years to have been her happiest and most exhilarating in the last decade.

She did four things equally well. First, she was a merciless and consistent critic of the Labour Government, exposing all its failures and shortcomings. Second, her criticism was never destructive, because it was expressed in the context of a positive alternative, which she explained and justified to the nation. Third, although a populist by nature, she recognised the need to change the climate of intellectual opinion in the country, particularly on the economy, and did so against considerable odds. Fourth, she worked hard to prepare the party for government, so that it would gain power and be able to use it effectively from the

outset, and bullied and cajoled her colleagues to do their home-
work as well. In all four areas her leadership was outstanding and
its rewards deserved. Throughout those years, she was honest in
admitting that things would not be easy and that her medicine
might well be unpalatable. But she insisted that both the diagnosis
and the remedy were correct and that nothing would deter her
from the prescription. This was courageous, and also appealing to
many people.

At the heart of the political debate was the economy, and at the
heart of the economic debate was the problem of inflation. To
deal with this problem, Margaret Thatcher proposed a policy that
became known as 'monetarism'*. The theory behind it was that
inflation was caused by printing too much money and that, by
limiting the money supply, inflation would be controlled, productivity and competitiveness increased, economic growth restored
and unemployment gradually reduced. This was the theory,
expounded by Milton Friedman, that attracted first Keith Joseph
and then Margaret Thatcher as its leading disciples. It formed the
foundation of the Conservative economic and political programme, developed and honed during the Opposition years. Was
there any disagreement about it within the Shadow Cabinet?

Yes and no. We were united in the belief that a decisive attempt
had to be made to break inflation and to make industry more
competitive. We all agreed that the objectives enshrined in
'monetarism' (low inflation, lower taxes, higher productivity,
more free competition, tighter control on Government expenditure) were desirable and need not be mutually exclusive. We
agreed that these policies had to be put forward singlemindedly if
they were to carry conviction at the election. But there were
doubts as to the universal truth of the theory and the rigidity with
which it should be implemented when the time came. Many of us
felt that no theory could take every factor into account and remain
right in all circumstances. That led us to question whether the
enforcement should be as rigid as the exposition. The seeds were
sown for a division between what I would term the theorists and
the pragmatists. Because the division related mainly to the imple-

---

* A fuller explanation of 'monetarism' – and of the reason for putting it in
inverted commas – is given in chapter eight.

mentation, it remained embryonic during the Opposition years. But when we won the 1979 election and Margaret Thatcher formed her Government, it took a more tangible form.

Margaret Thatcher made it plain, both in Opposition and as Prime Minister, that she would not moderate her policies. She felt the reason that successive Governments had failed to solve the problems was that they had compromised too easily, fudged the issues and lacked the courage to persevere. She insisted on the need to stick literally to the plan, come hell or high water.

Needless to say, both hell and high water duly materialised: hell in the form of the world recession, and high water in the form of the Cabinet wets*, who felt that this should make some difference to the economic strategy. The reason for our opinion was simple. The effects of 'monetarism' would always have included the closure of inefficient companies, a reduction in overmanning and the loss of unprofitable jobs: indeed, these were among the intentions of the policy. If world trade had been rising and the British economy growing, these effects need not have been too severe, because new and expanding companies would have filled the vacuum caused by the disappearing ones and would have provided new jobs to match those lost elsewhere. This is what was meant to happen. But the second explosion in oil prices in the summer of 1979 triggered the world recession and radically altered economic conditions. The problems were exacerbated by an overvalued pound – another effect of 'monetarism' – and, as a result, even successful companies struggled to stand still as world trade declined. It became apparent that companies and jobs would collapse on a far larger scale than previously envisaged and, more to the point, that these would not all be unviable companies or unprofitable jobs, but merely those unable to withstand intense short term pressure. The wets felt that this pressure should be relieved by Government action.

It is easy to understand the difficulties experienced by the Prime Minister at this point. She was quite clear as to what had to be done and, through no fault of her own, circumstances had changed radically almost as soon as she took office. I feel that

* I did not care for this epithet originally, but I am now resigned to it. I use it in this book as a recognised short-hand reference to a certain section of opinion within the Conservative Party at the moment.

Margaret Thatcher saw this crisis as a personal challenge to her resolve and became doubly determined not to give an inch on the economic strategy. Her rhetoric at the time reflected this.

But some of us saw things differently. We were still committed to the Government's economic objectives, but we believed that the world recession demanded a modified strategy to attain them. We also believed that, whether the strategy was modified or not, it would take much longer to achieve results than had been anticipated, and that it was vital to explain this to the nation and to reduce expectations in line with the new reality. That was the substance of the split between the wets and the 'monetarists' – indeed, that was the argument that led to the pejorative use of the term 'wet' in the first place. Led by the Prime Minister, the 'monetarists' won the day, if not the argument, and the strategy continued unaltered.

At this point, I will not go further into what could have changed and what might have happened if it had. The fact is that it did not. It is true that, despite the proclaimed rigidity, there were some compromises – such as the irony of Keith Joseph disgorging billions of pounds of tax payers' money to cover the losses of British Steel, British Leyland and others. But, on the important issues, the programme did not change. As a result, the money supply was contained with tolerable success, inflation duly fell, companies duly crashed, unemployment duly rose and productivity duly increased, but on a progressively lower manufacturing base.

Many Ministers were astonished by the rapid rise in unemployment and looked at the figures with disbelief. I was not one of them. Common sense dictated that 'monetarist' policies pursued during a severe recession would result in soaring unemployment. But, because this was not widely anticipated and because the other effects of the world recession upon industry and the economy were not foreseen, the strategy was not changed and the nation was not prepared for what was to happen. The Government developed tunnel vision, but there was no sign of light at the end of it. Its publicity still suggested that everything would shortly come right. Early in 1981, I began to make speeches alerting people to the fact that circumstances had changed and that the objectives would take longer to achieve. I warned that things might not come right for some time to come. I was attacked as a pessimist, but this is exactly what has happened.

By early 1982, the Government had run more than half its course and was faring disastrously in the opinion polls, with the Prime Minister's personal rating lower than it had ever been for any of her predecessors. Then the event occurred which was to transform the fortunes of the Government: Argentina invaded the Falkland Islands.

It is emphatically not the case that the Government looked upon this event as an opportunity to regain popularity. Indeed, the invasion of the islands and the events surrounding that disaster led to such a political crisis that it seemed doubtful at first whether the Government would survive. The whole operation was fraught with danger, military and political. In blunt terms, we evicted the invaders by force because no acceptable peace was available, and because both the Government and the overwhelming majority of the nation would not contemplate the thought of surrendering the islands. The success of the operation was due to superb military skills, resolute political leadership and the good luck that any such enterprise requires. But the consequence was a windfall for the Government.

The Falklands conflict restored the Government's popularity overnight and it was not substantially eroded until early 1984. Inflation continued to fall during 1982. The rise in unemployment became more gradual. An early election looked likely and in June 1983 it took place. At this time, the Labour Party was in disarray, as it had been since 1979, with an ineffective leadership, a damaging and largely incoherent manifesto and seemingly terminal divisions. The Alliance was too novel to be a serious contender so soon, and the Conservatives romped home by a vast majority. Since then, the Government has made a number of unforced errors but, as far as the main issues are concerned, little has changed. Inflation and unemployment seem to be more or less static, at least for the time being. The worst of the world recession appears to be over. Growth has returned to the economy. But big question marks hang over the nature and durability of the recovery, and over the means by which we can reduce unemployment, rebuild our industrial base, contain Government expenditure and create new wealth.

Margaret Thatcher made the most of the political opportunity created by the Falklands conflict, and she deserved her change of fortune. Politics are not just about managing the economy. They equally concern giving leadership at times of national crisis, and she provided good leadership in difficult circumstances. But, in addition, there was the second windfall of the state of the Labour Party and the way it fought the election. The effect of both factors is to make it difficult to say what the electorate's verdict would have been in other circumstances. My opinion is that, if the Labour Party had offered a credible alternative and if the Falklands War had never happened, the Conservatives would have lost the ensuing election.

Those of us in the Cabinet who wanted the rigours of 'monetarism' to be modified did so on several grounds: that it was economically vital in the changed circumstances, that it would be socially fairer, but also that it was politically necessary. We are now told that we were wrong on the last count in particular. I do not agree, since a true verdict was never delivered. The Government naturally claims that the 1983 landslide was a vindication of its policies, but my belief remains that it owed far more to General Galtieri and Michael Foot than it did to Milton Friedman. However, it also owed a lot to Margaret Thatcher.

People will say that it does not matter now: that history is full of might-have-beens, and that what actually happened is all that counts. But in fact it matters a great deal both to how one judges the 1979–1983 Government and to how one views the second term of office. Margaret Thatcher adopted a high-risk strategy and banked on using her persuasive powers to secure a second term. Had she failed, both her economic strategy and her political reputation would have been severely damaged, if not destroyed. From her viewpoint, the greatest fear in the first term was that a real, but as yet unapparent, economic success would result in political failure. If my viewpoint is accepted, the reality is that relative economic failure has been accompanied by fortuitous political success. I am therefore more inclined to view the 1983 election victory as an opportunity to correct the mistakes of the first term, rather than as a mandate to repeat them. I believe that many people in the country see things in this light and will judge the Government accordingly at the next election.

In making an evaluation of the Government's record over the last five years, I propose to deal only briefly with the economy at this stage. The subject is so important that it deserves detailed and separate consideration. A later chapter covers the economy in general and the theory and practice of 'monetarism' in particular. In this chapter, I am concerned with an overall assessment.

The successes of the Government are considerable and, since I am often accused of not acknowledging them, I would like to do so now. Ten achievements in particular should be put on the record.

First, Margaret Thatcher has returned decisive leadership to the forefront of British politics. She faces the problems honestly and presents her Government's policies clearly. She does not fudge the issues. She has clear objectives and clear means of achieving them. Even if one disagrees with some of them, it is difficult not to admire her decisiveness.

Second, she has shifted the political ground away from the leftward drift to Socialism. There is little doubt that she would view this as her main achievement: it is the thing she was most determined to do. The effects of that shift are now apparent. The new Labour Party leadership is defining its position largely on the Prime Minister's terms and with less reference to the traditional shibboleths of the left. David Owen feels it necessary to establish a position for the SDP that is overtly expressed in the context of Thatcherism. Even if the Government should fail at the next election, I doubt whether the succeeding Government would be able to repeal all its trade union and privatisation legislation. The spectrum of politics is and will remain as wide as ever, but the weight within the spectrum has shifted. The middle ground is a new middle ground, at least for the time being.

Third, for all her idealism, the Prime Minister has proved a political operator of consummate skill. Her success in making a virtue of unpopular measures has had the side-effect of branding anyone who disagrees with her as a spineless creature who seeks a cosy answer to any problem. The wets have been left wallowing in the water, and it would not surprise me if the Prime Minister sidled down to the beach and stole our clothes.

These achievements are all personal to Margaret Thatcher, accomplished with help from others but due mainly to the force of her personality. The remainder are more to do with the Government as a whole.

Fourth, the Government has successfully dealt with what it identified as the major problem – inflation. The promise was to cut it dramatically and this has been fulfilled. It is still higher than anyone would like, but it is lower than for a long time and, just as important, there is confidence that it is under control and will not erupt again amidst general surprise. One is inclined to forget how, for years, the inflation level bore little relationship to what the then Government had predicted. Not only was it rising, but it seemed that no one knew how to control it. It was a major achievement of Geoffrey Howe's to be seen to tame inflation: his forecasts of its future level were often spot-on and never over-optimistic, which did much for the credibility of the Government's economic policy. It even made it possible for the Government to declare shortly before the election that inflation would rise slightly during the year, and for people to believe exactly that: it would rise slightly. Had the preceding Government ever dared to suggest that inflation would rise slightly, everyone would have concluded – probably rightly – that it was about to rocket.

Fifth, industrial productivity has improved, although this owes more to the pressures of the recession than to positive Government action. The price of this success is that unemployment is higher than it would otherwise have been. However, the Government correctly stressed the need for higher productivity and, while I believe that more should have been done to tackle unemployment, I would not argue that this should have been at the expense of productivity.

Sixth, the Government's approach to trades union legislation has been an outstanding success. Established by Jim Prior and followed by Norman Tebbit and Tom King, the policy of gradual action to prevent abuses of union power has won consent from the country at large and even from many union members. This process has admittedly been aided by the recession and a subsequent weakening in the unions' bargaining position. However, since the union leaders extended their power for all they were worth when they held the advantage, they can hardly complain when others do the same, particularly when such action enjoys overwhelming public support. The Government has made good use of favourable circumstances.

Seventh, I believe that the privatisation programme has been a success. The role of the state in running industry has been curtailed. Several state monopolies have been broken. More effective management has been introduced in many of the nationalised industries. I do not agree with all aspects of the Government's approach to industry, but I believe that most of the privatisation programme has been sensible and will prove an enduring success.

Eighth, the policy of selling council houses to their tenants has been a great success. Not only is it in the best tradition of popular Toryism, but it has achieved the distinction of having virtually become the official policy of all four main parties, despite the hysteria that greeted its announcement.

Ninth, there has been a marked improvement in Britain's standing in the world. The credit for this is due to Peter Carrington. I do not refer only – or even mainly – to the settlement in Zimbabwe, although that was a considerable personal achievement, but to the whole way in which Britain has presented herself to the outside world, through both Government and diplomatic channels, and to how she has used her international influence. Such an achievement is impossible to measure, and many people may mistakenly take it for granted, but I doubt if there is a single overseas Government that does not have more respect for Britain now than five years ago.

Finally, I think that the Government's defence policy has greatly strengthened national security. This may be a contentious point but, leaving aside the nuclear issue, most people would surely accept that, if we are to be defended at all, we must be defended adequately. There is no point in being a half-hearted member of NATO. There is no point in having a defence system based on redundant weaponry. There is no point in being unable to withstand the perceived threat. The nuclear issue raises separate questions, to which I will return later in the book, but it remains my opinion that the Government has done a great deal to improve Britain's defences and to ensure that we play a positive role in the Western Alliance.

I believe that these are the Government's major achievements and many of them are attributable directly or mainly to Margaret Thatcher. Any Government would be proud to nail a comparable list of achievements to its mast and few have been able to do so in recent times.

But nothing is incapable of improvement. I retain the hope that instead of being branded as a 'Government critic', I will be recognised as someone who has consistently wanted to change some aspects of Government policy and approach, because I think it would be a great deal better both for the country and for the Government itself. My reservations concern three main areas: some aspects of policy, the public tone of the Government and its operational style. Although different, all three are connected and, in my opinion, stem from the same habit of tending to view everything in black and white.

The policies with which I disagree relate almost exclusively to the economic and industrial fields and to their social consequences. My conclusion is that 'monetarism' has encouraged a disproportionate emphasis on inflation, especially in the light of the world recession. In different circumstances such an emphasis could have been appropriate, but in reality it has exacerbated other economic problems, which a broader and more flexible strategy could have encompassed without threatening the control of inflation.

But, apart from questions of policy, I think that the public tone of the Government has often sounded unattractive and unsympathetic. It is the other side of the coin that I praised earlier. Conviction, determination and forceful logic can easily turn into dogmatism, inflexibility and insensitivity. As a result, people feel that the Government neither understands nor cares about them. This causes immense harm. Politicians have a duty to confront reality, whether it is comfortable or not. It is not vital to see everything at first hand, but it is significant that Margaret Thatcher has seldom visited those areas that have suffered most during the recession and that her election campaign of 1983 involved a studiously selected route through the more prosperous parts of the country. This has increased the sense that the Government cares only about part of the nation and not all of it. I do not believe that the Prime Minister lacks the courage to see problems for herself – she has made several trips to Northern Ireland at difficult times. Nor do I believe that she lacks feelings on such matters. Rather, I think she is afraid that her emotional reaction might tempt her to change her policies, in the same way that Michael Heseltine's emotional response to his inner-city visits after the 1981 riots undoubtedly affected his political response – quite correctly, in my opinion. Lack of sensibility is not the problem, but fear of it.

Politics dominated by emotion, however sincere, are inadequate. One can certainly kill with kindness and there is some truth in saying that British Governments have tended to do so. But the exclusion of compassion is equally wrong. There should be a balance between heart and mind. This does not always require policies to be changed, but it does require the human consequences of each policy to be considered, and at the very least this process affects the political tone. Far from being an abstract debating point, the presence or absence of a sympathetic tone has important practical consequences. If I am ill and go to my doctor, I hope that he will show care and concern for me. If that concern is apparent, I will much more readily accept an unpleasant cure or even the explanation that there is no cure. If it is not apparent, I will resent the cure or disbelieve the fact that there is none. I will feel that I do not matter to the doctor, and therefore that the diagnosis must be unconsidered and the prescription unreliable. I may be wrong, but that is how I will feel about it.

Regrettably, that is how many people feel about this Government. As a result, they have become suspicious of its policies and distrust some of its motives. This distrust is what the Labour Party is now feeding upon. It is hindering the Government's review of social funding, and may yet prevent radical reform from being implemented.

Two things have become confused in the public mind. The first is the attempt to cut Government spending. The second is the perceived attempt to reduce services. These two things need not be synonymous, and there is nothing to fear in the first, provided it is not accompanied by the second. There is no reason, in theory at least, why social services should not be provided more efficiently, without being reduced in scope or quality. Yet the unsympathetic tone of the Government has encouraged people to believe that any action it takes in the social service field will have both the purpose and the effect of reducing services. As a result, the Government is finding it far harder to implement radical and beneficial reforms than it need do, and it may even find that such reforms are impossible.

That is regrettable, because the problem of social funding will not go away and it must be faced. The Government is more concerned about the social services than its rhetoric suggests; it does not want to destroy them, as its opponents claim; it would like, as would we all, to preserve or improve the standard of services, but at a lower cost. This might involve a greater use of private finance, but my opinion is that this fact does not greatly concern people in itself. What most concern them are the quality of the services and their free availability to those who need them. Yet the point has now been reached where, if the Government even mentions the subject, people tend to assume the imminence of a wholesale cut in services. This view is supported by the capital that the Labour Party made out of the issue during the election, with the insinuation of a 'secret manifesto'. The accusation rang true with many people (and I am sure that Labour politicians believed it themselves), and the reason it rang true was that the tone of the Government had encouraged the belief that it did not care about people.

Such an assertion is incapable of proof, but I believe that if the Government had shown more visible concern from the outset, it would have been able to raise the possibility of reform in a spirit of national debate and without its motives being assaulted. Public opinion is starting to force the abandonment of radical policies. Some of these policies may be unacceptable in themselves; others are sensible, but are judged to be unacceptable before they have been considered, because the motivation is distrusted. This may not be justified, but it is understandable.

I think the Prime Minister recognises her vulnerability in this area, which is why she dislikes anyone raising such issues. But instead of trying to overcome the problem, she has run further away from it, back into the familiar black and white world where emotion is weakness, logic is strength, the policies are right, everything else is wrong and there is no alternative.

This brings me to my final criticism of the Government, which is that its style of operation has steadily become less flexible and more centralised. This process stems from the Prime Minister's tendency to think that she is always right. In turn, this leads her to believe that she can always do things better than other people, which then encourages her to try to do everything herself. The two consequences of this are, first, that central government now exercises direct control over more and more aspects of our lives and, second, that within the Government the Prime Minister exercises direct control over more and more Departments. Both developments conflict with the Government's stated beliefs in individual freedom and the danger of state intervention. The reason is simple. A belief in individual freedom is meaningless without a preparedness to allow other people to do things differently and, if necessary, to make mistakes.

The Prime Minister finds this fact hard to accept in practice. She would ideally like to run the major Departments herself and tries her best to do so – not just in terms of overall policy, but in strategic detail. This is neither practical nor desirable. Policy and decision-making require a full and careful understanding of many facts and considerations. Margaret Thatcher may have a retentive grasp of detail, but she cannot know enough to dictate the policy of each Department, as she has gradually discovered. Her response has been to expand the Downing Street staff to include experts in every major area, thus establishing a government within a government. In most cases, people have been chosen who reinforce her point of view rather than challenge it, which produces a greater rigidity of outlook than that encountered in the Civil Service.

I do not object to questioning the received wisdom or to encouraging a thorough argument about it, and no one can object to having a well-informed Prime Minister. But I object to a system that deliberately pits Downing Street against individual Departments, breeds resentment amongst Ministers and Civil Servants and turns the Prime Minister into a President. My concept of how a Government ought to work – and works best – is as a team of Ministers, fully responsible for their own Departments, led and directed by the Prime Minister and both collectively and individually accountable to Parliament. Indeed, this Government has been at its most effective when it has behaved in such a way, as it did when Jim Prior convinced Margaret Thatcher and the Cabinet of the need for a 'softly, softly' approach to union reform. However, I do not like the growing tendency for Ministers (and indeed Civil Servants) to be accountable to Downing Street, and only accountable to Parliament as agents of the Prime Minister.

This tendency affects not only specific Ministerial responsibilities, but collective Cabinet responsibility as well. The 1981 Budget was rigidly deflationary and thus highly controversial at a time of deep recession, yet the strategy behind it was never discussed in Cabinet and was only revealed to the full Cabinet on Budget Day itself. One can guess the reason: the Chancellor and the Prime Minister concluded that the Cabinet might well insist on some changes. But that is why the Cabinet exists – to make collective decisions on important issues that face individual Departments, and thus affect the Government as a whole. Collective responsibility is based on collective decision-making. Margaret Thatcher is not the first Prime Minister to circumvent her colleagues, nor will she be the last, but this habit is not the sign of a happy or healthy Government.

The drift to centralisation also affects the management of news. All Governments want a favourable Press and they go to considerable lengths to achieve one, but this Government goes further than most. Increasingly, Ministerial and Departmental press releases are channelled through Downing Street and suppressed or modified as necessary. The notorious leaks have emanated as much from Downing Street as from anywhere else. The Press receives a very good service from Number 10, which is perhaps why much of it is so uncritical. Perhaps it is also because newspaper magnates have a similar habit of seeing things in black and white. At any rate, some of the consequences have been hilarious. There was the occasion when the Prime Minister was earnestly assuring me of her support, while the Press reports that had led me to doubt it emanated directly from Downing Street. Later, when I made a rather critical speech at Oxford in November 1983, Downing Street felt it necessary to ring round Fleet Street and tell the Press that the speech was unimportant and should not be reported. Nobody in Fleet Street took much notice and the episode is more absurd than anything else, but it is a rather dubious way to behave.

More important, the centralising habit has now spread to major policy areas. It lies at the heart of the new Rates Bill presented to Parliament in January 1984. This is another instance of the Government backing down from necessary radical reform and adopting an expedient that replaces one iniquity with another. The objection to it has nothing to do with local government being universally good and efficient, nor with rates being a fair system. It isn't and they aren't. Nor is local government a blueprint for democracy in its present form, although it is better than no democracy at all. The objection is founded on the dangers of central government taking wide and undefined powers that could legally be used to do almost anything to local government. This is in striking contrast to the traditional Conservative philosophy of encouraging strong local government as an important element in our constitutional practice. Certainly no Conservative is much frightened about what Patrick Jenkin, the present Secretary of State, would do with such powers, but many of us are most apprehensive about what a future Government might do with them. Logic is being abandoned. A Government that set out with a mission to decentralise and to roll back the frontiers of the state is, in many respects, doing the precise opposite. The motive behind it is the belief that only by doing everything itself can the Government implement its policies, which is dangerously close to saying that the state always knows best.

So the tone and style of the Government disturb me as much as specific policy disagreements, not just because I dislike them, but because they are constraining the Prime Minister from achieving objectives that we both share. In evaluating the Government's record, I have been forthright in both praise and criticism. My conclusion is that the Government has achieved some notable successes and is infinitely to be preferred to the available alternatives. But it has not been as good as it could or should have been.

The Government's record is a stark contrast of black and white, a reflection of the attitudes that have driven it. Its credibility rests mainly on the assertion that the depths had to be plumbed before the heights could be scaled. From my position on the slope, the perspective is different. I believe that a moderated

economic strategy, a more sympathetic tone and a more relaxed
and open style would have avoided many of the problems without
jeopardising the successes.

TWO

A World View

'We can do noble acts without ruling earth and sea.' – ARISTOTLE

On the morning of Monday, 5 April 1982, like everyone else in the country, I was worrying about the serious events in the Falkland Islands and the tense debate in Parliament the previous Saturday. At midday, I received a telephone call from Downing Street asking me to come and see the Prime Minister at once. There she told me that Peter Carrington had resigned and asked me to take on the job of Foreign and Commonwealth Secretary.

It was a privilege to serve as Foreign Secretary and, once the rocks of the South Atlantic had been negotiated, a great pleasure as well. I have always tried to view politics from a perspective that extends beyond a narrow place and time, and have always felt that the post of Foreign Secretary is more than just another Government position: it embodies the continuity of British history and of our tradition as an outward-looking nation. Whatever our own difficulties, we have never been so myopic as to lose our sense of the world at large. This chapter therefore serves two purposes. It establishes a broad context of world affairs that gives perspective to later, more specific chapters. It also describes the outlook and attitudes that I brought to the job of Foreign Secretary and which formed the basis of my conduct of foreign affairs.

It is hard to condense such a huge subject into a few pages without losing the sense of scope. I want, therefore, to begin by charting the great changes that have affected world affairs this century, before considering Britain's role in this changed world and the major issues that now confront us. The most profound developments have been these three: the invention of nuclear weapons, the diffusion of world power and the revolution in communications.

As I am devoting a separate chapter to defence and nuclear disarmament, all I will say now is that the existence of weapons of such destructive power has made the world a far more dangerous place than ever before. The world has always seemed dangerous, since fear of the unknown is a permanent human condition, but the degree of that danger and the fear it breeds are now objectively greater. Antagonism between nations is eternal, but the risks attached to it – and especially the risk of tragic error – have increased immeasurably. We can never forget that the nuclear shadow looms over the discussion of all other issues.

That is the first great development. The second is the diffusion of world power. For many centuries, most major powers were contained within Europe. For much of that time, the world was not a single entity in practical terms and European power was largely self-contained. But from the sixteenth century onwards, Europe became outward-looking and expansive until, in the early years of this century, much of the globe either was or had been under its control – and especially under British control. Europe was the centre of the world.

The seeds of decline were sown in 1914. The tragedy of the First World War was an historical turning point. When it began, Europe was at the zenith of world affairs and might well have remained there. Major shifts in world affairs need a long time to take full effect, but ever since the First World War the relative power and influence of Europe has waned.

Some of the changes would have happened anyway. The sheer size and economic power of the United States would have ensured her pre-eminence. The demand for self-government by European colonies would still have been heard and would have proved irresistible. I do not suggest a static vision of European supremacy. But the probability is that, but for the First World War, there would have been no Hitler and no Second World War and that, but for these two wars, both the United States and the Soviet Union would have stayed far more isolationist than they have now become. In a changing context, Europe would have remained the centre of power. The two World Wars did more than divert European energies to a destructive and introverted end: they caused Europe to forfeit its moral capacity to direct the affairs of the world.

So, out of the morass of these conflicts, has developed the situation where America and Russia bestride the world as the two super-powers. The existence of two nations, both incomparably more powerful than any other, acting out their rivalry on the canvas of the world, is a new phenomenon. The irony is that both these nations used to be, and perhaps inherently still are, more isolationist than expansionist in temperament.

The evidence of all but recent history suggests that Russian expansionism is by nature regional and not global. The impetus was towards a gradual enlargement of the country's borders, rather than domination of the world beyond. But that history has been overshadowed by two events. The first was repeated invasion from Europe, which brought appalling casualties and a suffering that is almost impossible to conceive. No wonder the Russians have learnt to mistrust other nations and should want adequate defences to prevent the same thing happening again. The second event was the domination of the Russian spirit by the alien ideology of Marxism. This doctrine is far more expansionist than the character of the Russian people. It is the fear of this doctrine that has forced the West to bury its own differences and has persuaded the United States to carry the burden of resistance for the free world.

The Americans have made a courageous entry into world affairs, taking the lead for the West within a remarkably short time, without any prior experience. One can question how well they have done it, but one can also question how well Britain did it when she had the responsibility. Nor should we forget that it was Europe's inability to defend its own freedoms and democracies that twice drew the Americans to our assistance. Whatever the present tensions, we would all feel even less secure if America had not taken such a burden upon herself.

Thus there are two super-powers, with very different histories and from very different continents, dominating the surface of the globe and now even vying with each other in the far reaches of the universe, just seventy years after the old powers of Europe plunged themselves into a war from which they have never fully recovered. But, although world power is now more concentrated, it is paradoxically more diverse. The spread of economic growth and Europe's withdrawal from its colonies have together created scores of new, thriving and independent nations. These countries may not possess great power, but they have the means – and some have used them – to cause great instability in the world. In this way, as the dominance of the super-powers has grown, so their control has diminished. Both developments amount to one of the profound changes, not just of this century, but of all time. Yet I believe that the third change – the revolution in communications – which has been simultaneous with the shift in world power, may even rival it in importance.

The world of our forefathers was a large and unknown place. A town fifty miles away was distant. Most provincial Englishmen never went to London, let alone to Europe. The wider world existed in maps and atlases, and in the adventures of a few, whose written words stirred the imagination of many. Because there was little knowledge, there was little presumption to understanding. Now we can transport ourselves across the world in hours and bring its images to our homes in seconds. We rely no longer on the excitement of our imagination by the written word, but on the vivid moving pictures of celluloid and satellites. All the while, experts and analysts present and dissect the issues of the day before our eyes.

This is a staggering change. It is a leap in human development of incalculable dimensions. The benefits it has brought of greater knowledge and an ability to reduce the vastness of the world to a comprehensible scale are evident. But for every gain there is a loss, and I wonder if we have contemplated the problems that the media revolution has caused.

The fact that we know so much more about world events has compressed time as well as space. Previously, wherever peace prevailed, each country could pursue its own course in its own time. The world has never been at a single, unified stage of development, nor should it need to be. This is not a patronising British view: after all, when Athens flourished, we were the barbarians of the age. The variety in the world is a cause for wonderment and not for censure. But that variety has now become difficult to honour. We judge other countries by the standards of our own place and time and fail to appreciate that the circumstances are different. When we see barbarism in the world around us, we should recognise it as such, but we have no right to expect or to impose uniformity. Such an attempt might threaten our own liberties more than it would extend them to others. Time is the most mysterious of dimensions and I fear that we are losing our sense of its mystery.

The instant availability of news also conceals the subtle difference between factual knowledge and understanding, which we confuse at our peril. We may know how many missiles the Russians have, how many tanks, how many ships, how many planes; but this knowledge is a mere prelude to arms control. For that, we need to understand the human truths: the history, the feelings, the beliefs. The physical facts are never enough.

There is always a danger that understanding will diminish as factual knowledge increases. The images we see on our televisions reflect only the symptoms and consequences of a problem. To understand the causes, whether in the South Atlantic in 1982 or in the Middle East now, requires a degree of study that goes far beyond either the desire of most people to apply or the time at their disposal to do so. When we see world events portrayed on the screen and described by commentators, that does not lead to understanding, but only to an emotional reaction and the acquisition of casual knowledge.

Another effect of modern communications is the casting of an international spotlight on every dispute. This pressure is far more severe in the West than in totalitarian countries, where the absence of a free media enables the state to extinguish the spotlight at will. But elsewhere, any significant event is on the screens in most capitals within minutes. What would once have been a local dispute now attracts scores of nations taking sides. Everyone is involved and feels the need to be involved. The spotlight acts as a magnet for the malcontent and gives sordid deeds the glow of renown. Even those who do not seek it are sought by it; the world takes sides and the dispute moves further from solution.

The cumulative effect of these pressures on the two super-powers is considerable. As the momentum of any event builds up, it becomes very hard for America or Russia to stand on the sidelines. Disputes with no real importance outside their own area acquire a disproportionate significance. The Falklands War is one of the few recent instances where neither super-power was directly involved. But, even then, the United States was active on our behalf behind the scenes, while the Russians tried to interfere in the region and acquire a foothold in South America. This process adds to the dangers of the world, yet at present it seems inevitable. America and Russia watch each other like hawks across the globe, and the power of each will be invoked in almost every conflict. Their respective motives are, in my view, quite different. The Soviet Union is governed by a dirigiste régime, which seeks to impose its brutal will, not only on its immediate neighbours, but anywhere else that it sees an opportunity to do so. By contrast, the United States has no such expansionist intent, and intervenes only – if sometimes with dubious justification – to prevent Soviet encroachment. But the fact of global involvement remains the same, and this is partly the consequence of the revolution in communications.

I do not blame the media for these problems; nor do I regret the emergence of modern communications. Information and knowledge are priceless gifts, which enrich us in many ways. Understanding is still more priceless, but maybe that will emerge in time. This development, together with the invention of nuclear weapons and the diffusion of world power, has made today's world almost unrecognisable to nineteenth century eyes. These changes form the setting for British foreign policy in the modern world.

Twenty years ago, Dean Acheson described Britain as a nation 'that has lost an empire and has not yet found a role'. Seven years on, Alan Bennett summarised it thus: 'To let. A valuable site at the cross-roads of the world. At present on offer to European clients. Outlying portions of the estate already disposed of to sitting tenants. Of some historical and period interest. Some alterations and improvements necessary.' These expressions reveal the inevitable confusion which many people felt about our international role in the post-war period. In the space of twenty years, we fought a world war of tragic proportions, watched as two super-powers eclipsed us in its aftermath, and presided over the dismemberment of our own Empire. A shock of this magnitude needs time to be absorbed. Now we have come to terms with the changes, we can set about a realistic appraisal of what is possible, with neither useless regret for the past nor vain hope for the future.

The most striking feature of the new world is that, despite all the changes, it is remarkably similar to the old one. The acquisition of power, the drive to war and the desire for peace, the fears and misunderstandings between nations: they exist now as they did a hundred years ago, as they have existed through the ages. We may have learnt to harness the earth's resources to the benefit of humanity, but we have not learnt to do the same with human instincts and emotions. That is why Britain's interests remain unaltered. They can be summarised in three words: peace; stability; trade. And they all go together. We want to live peaceably as a prosperous trading nation. We have gone to war in two circumstances: when an overweening power has threatened the stability of Europe, or when either our trading routes or peoples under our protection have been attacked. But our objective has always been to achieve a peaceful and stable world, in which our trade can flourish.

As in the past, British foreign policy must use all available means to achieve this objective. Today, this entails the recognition of two facts: that our influence is greater than our power, and that both will be more effective if they are used in conjunction with other nations and not in isolation. Put briefly, we need to use our vast experience and considerable influence, in partnership with others, to build bridges of understanding that will lead the world towards greater peace and stability.

There is much nebulous talk of 'British influence', but it can certainly be defined, even if it cannot be measured. First, there is a mass of goodwill towards this country, based on respect for our history, experience and judgment. We have friends around the world who believe that, whatever differences may lie in the past, we are a force for peace. Second, there is the tangible legacy of our Empire. In every continent, there are forms of government and justice that originated in this country. Finally, there is the asset of the English language, the most widely-spoken tongue in most parts of the world. These are all priceless international assets.

We cannot afford to view such assets purely as a legacy of the past: they will survive only if they are constantly developed. That is why I attach such importance to the Diplomatic Service, to organisations like the British Council, and to independent bodies like the BBC. Apart from its vital role in disseminating the English language, the BBC is by far the most respected broadcasting service internationally, because of its reputation for truth and integrity. It is a source of pride – and in some ways of regret – to know that many people listen to the BBC when they want to know what is happening in the world, because they do not trust their own media to tell them. Together, all three bodies extend our influence in a unique way. They may not enhance British power – nor should they, for that matter – but they greatly enhance the respect in which we are held. It is vital that enough funds are made available to maintain, and if possible to expand, the work of these bodies, and I fought successfully to prevent their erosion when I was Foreign Secretary.

However, influence and respect are not enough: they have to be turned to practical account. Although we can do this partially through our own efforts, we can do it more effectively with others. In particular, there are three groups – leaving aside the United Nations, which plays a disappointingly weak role in events – through which our influence can be extended and our interests pursued: NATO, the EEC and the Commonwealth. All three are vital to Britain, whatever some might think. The next two chapters cover NATO and the EEC, but the Commonwealth is no less significant.

When one knits together such diverse problems in the world as race, poverty, the polarity of the super-powers, the environment and a lack of understanding between nations, the value of the Commonwealth becomes apparent. I have always attached the greatest importance to it and was particularly glad to be able to give clear expression to this while Foreign and Commonwealth Secretary. Some people say that the Commonwealth is an historical anachronism, representing no real coalescence of mutual interests or beliefs. Exactly. That is why it is so valuable. Precisely because it does not need to exist, precisely because nobody is compelled by immediacy to belong to it, precisely because it is not buoyed up by expedient self-interest, it can only survive if all its members approach it in a spirit of human understanding that transcends temporal divisions. Not the least of the debts we owe to our Royal Family is for its dedication to sustaining the values of the Commonwealth, despite all pressures. The Commonwealth, quite literally, is irreplaceable and the Royal Family recognises this in a way that not all politicians do.

Foreign policy must be based on national self-interest, and I see nothing wrong in that. But the perception of self-interest must in turn be based on a broad and long term view of events. A narrow approach that heightens conflict and tension for the sake of a dubious short term gain is harmful and self-defeating. Immediate objectives must be balanced with wider ones. The ultimate self-interest of every country lies in a mutual understanding between nations, tolerance and respect for different cultures and values, and a voluntary acceptance of the reality of interdependence. As Foreign Secretary, I certainly pursued immediate British objectives as strongly as I could, while never – I hope – losing sight of our broader goals.

With this in mind, I want to consider the major issues of today and tomorrow under three headings: political, economic and environmental. The two most serious political conflicts concern the Middle East and Central America. As I write, the circumstances of both are changing almost daily. It would therefore be futile to attempt a detailed commentary on either in the course of a book. However, some overall comments are necessary, and are likely to remain appropriate for some time to come, even if the details change.

The Middle East conflict involves two separate problems. The first is rooted in the creation of the state of Israel and the effects of that on the Arab world. The second is rooted in the upsurge of Moslem fundamentalism. Of the two, I feel that the second poses the greater medium term threat, though the first attracts more headlines. The danger of both is enhanced by the double strategic importance of the area: economically as the major source of the world's oil, and geographically because it is adjacent to the Soviet Union.

The first conflict has either simmered or erupted since the state of Israel was created. Whilst acknowledging her need for security, I feel that Israel tends to confuse this legitimate concern with a sense of insecurity that borders on the paranoid. The Arab countries resent the fact that she has repeatedly extended her borders at their expense. Most of them accept that Israel should have security, but not with her present boundaries; the 120 million Arabs between the Atlantic and the Gulf will never find the present position acceptable. The Israeli invasion of the

Lebanon in June 1982, which occurred during my time at the Foreign Office, was a damaging escalation of the conflict. The Israelis judged it to be necessary but, as I made clear at the time, I do not agree. Whatever the justification, this step was bound to make the basic problem harder to solve. It also brought about the active involvement of the United States in the Lebanon, which had hardly seemed possible a short time before.

To be blunt, the internal situation in the Lebanon is of little intrinsic importance to the West. What matters is the stability of the whole region. This has not been enhanced by America's involvement in the Lebanon, nor by her 'strategic understanding' with Israel in November 1983, nor by the vain attempt to freeze Russia out of a role in negotiations. Attention has been diverted from the problems of the Palestinians and the extent of Israel's borders, which is where it should be concentrated.

In September 1982, President Reagan produced a plan that owed a great deal to the views of Britain and other European nations, as set out in the Venice Declaration. It was based on the twin principles of security for Israel and autonomy for the Palestinians, possibly in association with Jordan. It was a good vehicle for direct negotiations between the Arabs and Israelis. Arab leaders held a conference at Fez later that month, which did not rule out such negotiations. Israel, by contrast, not only rejected the Reagan Plan out of hand, but continued to extend her illegal occupation of the West Bank, to the further provocation of the Arabs. Progress depended on Israel modifying her position, which in turn depended on the exertion of American pressure on Israel. This need was urgent, since each passing week brought the American Presidential Election nearer, and made the chances of success slimmer. I spoke often on these lines to George Shultz, US Secretary of State, and also to Vice-President George Bush during his visit to London in February 1983. But the Reagan Plan was not vigorously pursued, and instead America concluded an agreement with Israel. In the light of subsequent events, this whole approach seems even more mistaken now than it did at the time.

The second Middle East conflict, born out of Moslem fundamentalism, was epitomised by the Iranian revolution and is now apparent in the Iran–Iraq war. The first conflict is dangerous enough, but this one has two added dimensions: it poses a growing threat to the West's oil supplies and it has a profound impact on the whole Arab world. Any upheaval in the area, but especially one that touches the conscience of all Moslems, threatens the stability of moderate Arab nations and thus Western interests. Nor can the possibility of direct Soviet involvement in Iran be ignored, even though the Russians know that, if they were to chance their arm in the Gulf, the Americans would be bound to react. The danger undoubtedly exists of the germ of a third world war starting in the Middle East, and that is why recent events both in the Lebanon and between Iran and Iraq have implications of a most dangerous kind. Even without such a catastrophe, one can only assume that the Middle East will remain in crisis over the next few years. The strongest Western lead is called for if the deterioration is to be arrested.

On a different scale and in a different way, Central America is equally important, because of its proximity to the United States. Through the medium of Cuba, the Soviet Union has been able to infiltrate more arms into the region and to exploit its endemic instability. If Russia is allowed to set up puppet Marxist régimes throughout Central America, apart from doing nothing to improve life for the people, a direct threat will be posed to the United States, which is precisely the Soviet intention. America cannot possibly tolerate this, nor should we expect our most powerful ally to be exposed to such a danger. The same process has been attempted in parts of the Caribbean and was the reason for the American invasion of Grenada. Developments on that island had to be stopped, even if many of us regretted that the usual close consultation between London and Washington failed completely on this occasion.

The urgent need is to bring stability to Central America. In the short term, this necessitates bolstering some thoroughly distasteful régimes, while putting pressure on them to moderate their worst excesses, before – one hopes – more moderate governments can take over. I dislike this expedient as much as anyone, but no one has yet persuaded me of any alternative except to stand back and allow the untrammelled advance of Soviet control. I accept the view that for the West to give support to corrupt or repressive régimes will ultimately diminish both its moral authority and its political strength. But speeches for democracy are inaudible amidst the chatter of machine-guns, and the practice of democracy cannot begin until the guns are silenced and stability is assured. When powerful interests are at work destabilising countries, it is not surprising that the language of the bullet prevails.

The wisest way of resolving the problem of Central America lies in co-operation between the United States and the countries most involved. The Contadora Group (consisting of Mexico, Venezuela, Colombia and Panama) is a major factor in the area and could play a vital role in helping to secure stability.

Turning to more general areas of conflict, racial differences are perhaps the greatest problem. For many years, South Africa has been the main focus of this conflict, crystallising everyone's deepest emotions on race. Both sides have displayed an intransigence which, while it may gratify a sense of moral righteousness, does nothing to help solve the problem. In such a highly charged atmosphere, profound emotions are inevitably engaged. At this point, we all have a choice. We can allow our emotions full rein, in which case confrontation is inescapable, or we can widen our perceptions through a more rational approach to the problem.

To begin with, we should discard all hypocrisy and double standards. However repressive the South African régime, it is no more repressive than dozens of other régimes, from the Soviet Union downwards. This fact does not excuse South Africa, but it is reason enough not to make her the sole inmate of an isolation ward. The habit of doing so is both intellectually and morally dishonest. We should either boycott all such nations or none of them, which is why I at least respect those who argue that we should ostracise all governments that offend substantially against our principles, whatever the material damage to ourselves. I do not, however, agree with them.

I can see no point in empty moral gestures. I am also profoundly sceptical of the notion that revolutions benefit anybody, least of all those they are meant to benefit. I want to see peaceful change in South Africa and I am prepared to use pressure to encourage it, but only in a way that is practical and that takes account of Britain's economic interests. Our commercial links with South Africa are considerable; they create wealth for Britain, and they are one of the few levers we possess with which to pressurise the

South African Government. I regret the imposition of sporting and cultural boycotts, as I do not believe in shutting down human contact; but the exertion of influence through economic and political contacts is a legitimate tactic. I am not ashamed of a policy that involves trading with South Africa – or with any other such régime – on the one hand, and encouraging the cause of peaceful change on the other. My experience is that this approach is more likely to achieve the twin objectives of political reform and continued trade.

Having said that, I am not sanguine about the immediate prospects for change. If used wisely, South Africa's current success in neutralising her neighbours should create a breathing space for her Government to begin the process of internal reform. I fear it is more likely to be used as an excuse to do nothing. If so, on their own heads be it. The experience of history is that undemocratic Governments which refuse legitimate and necessary reform are eventually overthrown, and that this process is not inhibited by the fact that those who were previously oppressed seldom become less oppressed in consequence. One day this will happen in South Africa, unless there is substantial change. In that event, I will shed no tears for the leaders of South Africa, but we may all need to fear for her people and for the global effects of such an upheaval.

Whatever happens in South Africa or elsewhere, the race problem cannot be 'solved'. We can alter many things, but we cannot change the race to which we belong. What matters is how we approach such an emotive issue. If we allow our irrational side to govern our whole personality, we will fail as surely as if we deny that irrational side altogether. A subjective emotional response is not invalid, but it is not enough. The more we indulge in our own emotions, the more we isolate ourselves from those of others. We become less able to discern our common humanity and we accentuate an unjustified sense of superiority. There is no other issue where this emotional barrier is so huge, nor the need to dismantle it so great.

All the problems I have discussed are likely to remain with us in the future, but the most important question is the prospect of change in the balance of world power. Over the centuries, that balance has altered radically. Some changes have been sudden and drastic; others have involved a gradual tilt to an existing balance. But, over a long sweep of time, the centre of power has moved through different countries and continents. This movement will not stop. Over the last forty years, we have become accustomed to a stable, if dangerous, situation with America and Russia as the two super-powers, but this cannot last indefinitely.

If either declines, I believe – and of course hope – that it will be Russia rather than America, for a number of reasons. As a democracy, America has a greater human strength running through society than Russia has under a totalitarian régime. As a younger nation, it is clear that America has more vitality. I believe that the historical tide of Marxism is already on the turn. I think that Western Europe and the rest of the free world will prove more durable allies for America than her own satellites will for Russia. The economic strength of American capitalism is considerable. Russia has a host of internal problems that dwarf the West's difficulties. All these factors weigh in America's favour.

In the course of time, circumstances could arise when the yoke of Marxism will vanish and the spirit of the people will be liberated in Russia, Poland and throughout Eastern Europe. In that sense, I take a long term view of optimism. But in the meantime, the West must maintain both its nerve and its strength. We must look after ourselves and leave events behind the Iron Curtain to evolve at their own pace, confident that Marxism will eventually collapse under its own weight and fulfil the historical fate it has always predicted for capitalism.

Whatever happens in Russia, we are likely to witness the ascendancy of Asia, and specifically of the Far East. The region has a formidable record of industrial achievement. It has a huge population, which is growing rapidly. It has a great many natural resources. When one sees what has happened in Japan, and what is happening in countries like Korea and Taiwan, an increase in influence seems certain. My feeling, therefore, is that the twenty-first century will see the dominance of the Far East. The major question is the role that China will play in this process. At the moment, she naturally wants to extend her influence, but her ambitions do not appear to stretch further. However, that position could change.

All this makes it even more important for Europe to retain an influence on events. Even though substantial European power was lost some while ago, the fact that both Russia and America have always had strong European links and are both Northern Hemisphere nations has enabled Europe to remain an area of disproportionate significance. The rise of the Far East would change that situation, along with many other things. If world power does shift in this way, it will have been instigated more by economic than by political factors, and it is the economic issues of the world upon which I would now like to comment.

The shrinking of the globe through communications is forcing the whole world to come together, however much politics pull it apart. The other unifying factor is the realisation of how reliant we are on each other economically. The concept of interdependence between nations is not a platitude: it is the reality. This fact is reflected in the emergence of regional groupings, which is one of the more encouraging features of the world scene. Everywhere, nations are finding that the world is too complex to allow them to solve their problems in isolation. It is also very difficult for small countries to have any influence on affairs, unless their opinions are voiced as part of a larger group.

This movement originated in Europe with the European Economic Community. Now there are many such groups: the Gulf Co-operation Council in the Middle East, the Association of South East Asian Nations, the Contadora Group and other groups in the Caribbean, the Pacific and West Africa. In fact, there are very few countries that now operate on their own. China is the obvious example, but increasingly an isolated one. These groups are constructive and, since any co-operation requires give and take, they help us all to appreciate other points of view. In that way, they make a major contribution to stability.

The reality of interdependence means that no country can recover from the world recession on her own. Each will have a more prosperous future only if others do likewise. It is a failure to grasp this fact that has led to the recent clamour for protectionism in Britain and elsewhere. In many ways it is understandable. The human and social consequences of the recession, coupled with the growth of foreign competition, encourage people to believe that, if Britain put up the barriers, she could protect domestic industries and secure both employment and prosperity. In fact we would secure neither: we would be starting a trade war in which we would feel the hardship more than most other countries. Britain is and has always been a trading nation. Trade is the life-blood of our economy. It must be based, as it always has been, on the premise that if we wish to trade with other countries, they must be allowed to trade with us.

This issue need not be considered in theory alone. In my own lifetime, after 1930, experience confirmed the fact. Everyone put up trade barriers, thinking this would ease the Depression. The result was a disaster, and the recovery that followed the slump of the 1930s was partly achieved by the opposite policy of free trade. A prosperous world cannot exist on a protectionist basis and the drift towards it must be resisted. We should do better to turn our energies from protectionism to competitiveness. Not the least reason to do so is the growing challenge from other parts of the world. Existing sources of competition will increase and they will be joined by new sources. Aid and technological assistance will help to develop the poorer economies, and their industries will form part of a worldwide competition in many markets.

This leads to the question of poverty and the Third World. Here again, communications illuminate the paradox that the more we feel a part of one world, the more the discrepancies in that world become apparent. Once more we become entangled in the problems of time and space. Time is not equal throughout the world, nor is space, nor are individuals. Beyond the basic equality of humanity, all things are different. It would not be fruitful, or even possible, to share the rewards of the industrialised countries equally around the world; but it is vital, both in human terms and because of the mutual dependence of nations, to help poorer countries to overcome their immense problems and ultimately to share in a universal prosperity.

Britain has a special responsibility in this process. We have brought nearly fifty countries to independence, many of them facing the most intractable difficulties. We have always attached great importance to aid programmes: in helping with investment, with technological skills and with economic development, as well as with the relief of emergencies. The need is almost limitless, and our resources are not, so we can never avoid the fact that there is more to be done. I would like to see more joint ventures between Western nations and both the World Bank and private industry to help to accelerate the process. We are all part of the same world and we have to work together.

More education about the role and effectiveness of aid is required in the West, and the kind of enquiry undertaken by the Brandt Commission is invaluable in providing a rationale for these programmes. We must also do everything we can to further contact and training. Britain has a great tradition of welcoming overseas students, and this is a wise policy. Not only do the students, and thus their countries, benefit from the training, but they are far more likely to look to Britain politically and commercially in the future if they are familiar with the country and her people. This tradition was overturned by drastic cut-backs in 1979, which were damaging and short-sighted. I was determined to reverse this process and, after much argument, succeeded in restoring some of the cuts.

Bridging the gap to the Third World, the growing interdependence of nations, the increase in competition: these are the main economic issues of the future. For the present, it remains the priority to bring the current world recession to an end. There is no easy way to do this, least of all through protectionism. I would like to see more political will and imagination from the leading industrialised nations in tackling the underlying problems. The present fragile recovery is vulnerable to a relapse. The summit meeting of industrialised nations, which takes place every summer, has not solved these problems and is in danger of becoming a ritual. Meetings should take place when they need to, which in present conditions may be more often than once a year.

The most encouraging sign for recovery lies in the stability of oil prices. The two vast increases in the price of oil in 1973 and 1979 temporarily enriched the oil producing countries, but impoverished the rest of the world and helped to trigger off the recession. However, these events forced us to explore new ways of saving energy and also to develop new sources of energy. In retrospect, the oil producers overplayed their hand. The world now has a massive reserve of energy and this fact should help to stabilise prices and provide one precondition for the recovery, assuming that the Iran–Iraq war does not spark off an even worse set of problems.

The final issues I want to consider concern the environment. Rather than examine individual aspects of the subject, I would prefer to put the debate in a broader context. It seems to me that when, in the seventeenth century, civilisation turned finally away from the natural, instinctive world of the ancients towards the rational, logical world of the moderns, this was one of the profound changes of human history. The repercussions of that change have been enormous, both in the benefits they have conferred and in the problems they have created. One repercussion has been the development of science and technology, from which have stemmed equally the wonder of modern medicine and the horror of nuclear arms. Another repercussion has been the cult of material values, from which have stemmed equally the rapid rise in real living standards and the corresponding rise in human greed.

The environmental arguments of today are replaying these ancient themes. The environmentalists remind us of the negative side of these developments; the scientists of the positive side. Behind the latter's argument is the assumption that there is no problem science has created which it cannot cure. Behind the former's argument is the belief that such confidence is arrogant, unjustified and dangerous. So how should one view it? Is man an adept at harnessing the boundless resources of the earth for his own improvement, or is he a locust who is turning his only world into a wilderness?

Whatever answer one gives to this question, it has to be personal: general political principles do not apply. My own view is that one cannot divorce the positive achievements of science from the negative ones: the two go together. We therefore need to balance the competing needs of material progress and wider values, spiritual as well as environmental, rather than to make what I see as a false choice between them. We cannot ignore the fact that the earth's resources are finite. We cannot, through a one-sided development of the scientific mind, allow the world itself to become unbalanced. But if we let a hatred of science and industry lead us in the opposite direction, we will just as surely diminish ourselves. To balance the drive of science with the needs of our environment is an extremely difficult task, but that is what we most need to do.

At present, I feel that the balance is tilted away from the environment and I concede that few politicians have devoted enough time or thought to the issue. Part of the difficulty is that to tackle such problems involves action within one's own country, within other countries and between all countries. Such co-operation is hard to achieve.

Ultimately, this issue lies in the hands of the people, at least in the democracies of the world. The protection of the environment demands material sacrifice. Politicians can and should take a lead, but public pressure has always inclined us to the side of materialism. If we are to lean the other way, we need the signal of a widespread preparedness to pay the price involved. There are signs, particularly in West Germany, that this might be happening. Certainly, throughout the Western world, there is a greater understanding of the issues and a greater interest in them. That in itself is encouraging. But it is a sobering thought that, for all the so-called materialism of the West, many of the worst abuses of the environment occur in the Soviet bloc.

When I look at the state of the world, I feel a sense of both optimism and pessimism. The sources of pessimism are familiar and need no repetition. The sources of optimism are the feeling that humanity has at times shown the capacity to learn from its mistakes and to transcend its differences, the knowledge that there are enough people of goodwill who are dedicated to this task, and the belief that the countries of Europe, and Britain in particular, can make an enormous contribution to the world. In the course of this chapter, I have described my own attitude to events and to the conduct of British foreign policy. I believe strongly in the need for a broad and enlightened view of self-interest and not in a narrow self-defeating nationalism.

The divisions that bedevil the world are also its glory. Despite the advance in communications, the world is still infinitely diverse. It embraces a wealth of different civilisations, different cultures, different attitudes, different beliefs. All nations are different. Within nations, all people are different. There are three ways that we, as individuals or as nations, can react to this diversity as it is encountered in others. We can either suppress it by forcing a bogus uniformity on nature. That has been the hallmark of tyranny down the ages and it finds expression today in the Marxist régimes of the Soviet bloc. Or we can stare uncomprehendingly at the diversity, fearing it, unable or unwilling to take a step forward to meet it, with both sides reduced to uttering slogans across the great divide. This, alas, has been the habit of most people at most times in history.

Or we can take that step forward across the divide, not seeking to suppress or to be suppressed, but only to understand, and in that moment of understanding to find the common humanity that transcends and unites diversity, yet does not diminish it.

This last choice is the only hope for the world. The conduct of foreign policy, based on human contact across the world, is a means of pursuing that hope. It is not the only means. Anything that advances understanding of other viewpoints, and especially human contact between people of different nations, is a step towards the ultimate goal. That is why diplomacy cannot be measured in its effectiveness. Because its aim is human understanding, its values are feeling values, tonal and not absolute.

I am under no illusions about the realities of British power in the world. But although power bestows influence, influence does not depend exclusively on power. The noonday sun is powerful and it burns. The evening sun exercises its influence in a different way. It is mellow and mature. It bathes the world in a benign light. Whether we like it or not, Europe is one of the oldest living civilisations. Now is the time to make full use of all we have learned. I look forward, not to the twilight, but to watching the rich sun of the Western world temper the newer lights around us with the warm glow of its experience.

THREE

Defence and Disarmament

'Fear is stronger than arms.' – AESCHYLUS

The arms race is a marathon in which there are no winners. Russia is in the throes of the biggest military build-up in her peacetime history. America has responded in kind. Cruise missiles are in Britain and are imminent elsewhere in Europe. Pershing II missiles are in Germany. Billions of roubles, dollars and pounds go to bloat the nuclear arsenal, while half the world starves. The stockpile of weapons could destroy the world many times over, as if once were not enough. Meanwhile, until recently, the leaders of the two super-powers have stood on their respective sides of the abyss, hurling slogans at each other. All these facts assault our emotions and threaten our reasoning.

And yet we live at peace.

We are saddled with this contradiction, beset by conflicting fears. Western fear of the Soviet Union has prompted the growth of Western armaments. Soviet fear of the West has prompted the growth of Soviet armaments. Mutual fear of the armaments themselves has deterred their use. The fear that they will be used has given birth to unilateralism. The fear of nuclear blackmail has encouraged multilaterlism. In our different ways, we are trying to come to grips with our fear of a monster that our fears have created, still uncertain as to which of the fears are justified.

Nobody in Britain can or should be unaffected by the nuclear debate: it is too close to all of us. It is closer for politicians, who have to take the decisions. It is closer still for Ministers, like myself, who have had specific responsibility for nuclear policy. I was Secretary of State for Defence when the decisions were taken on both Cruise missiles and Trident. Never have I lived so near to an issue for so long a period, and seldom have I needed to be more certain of my actions. This chapter is therefore more than one man's view on a major issue: it reflects the reasoning of someone who took the responsibility, and will always bear part of it, for two vital and controversial decisions.

Where any weapons are concerned, the onus of proof must lie on those who advocate their possession. Governments cannot take the attitude that a military capability is a proven necessity, needing no further justification, and that the responsibility is on those that think otherwise to prove their case. Nobody disputes that in an ideal world there would be no need for anyone to bear arms. In that case, if a Government believes there is such a need in practice, it has a continuing duty to explain and to justify that need. It is in such a spirit that I approach the issue.

The question of national defence is not primarily to do with nuclear weapons, even if they are its most dominant feature today. In the first instance, it is to do with the principle of defending oneself at all.

There are only two reasons to possess a weapon: to attack somebody else or to defend oneself against attack, which includes deterring attack in the first place. The latter has been and remains the only inducement to Britain to maintain her armed forces. We are not an aggressive nation. We have no intention of instigating hostilities. Our desire is to live in a peaceful, stable world. The only justification for our defence policy is to promote peace and stability, not to jeopardise them. The means by which we achieve this, or seek to achieve it, is a process of logic in which I firmly believe and which I want to justify.

The validity of any process of logic depends on the truth of its premise: if the premise is false, logic leads inexorably to madness. Since many people believe, with some reason, that the world's arms policies are indeed leading rapidly to madness, we must establish whether the reason is a false premise, or false logic, or some other factor altogether.

The premise on which any defence policy is based is a belief that self-defence is justified. Without that belief, there is no need to have a defence policy at all. This is the pacifist view, and it embodies the principle that nothing is worth fighting for. Pacifists have always had to endure the taunt of cowardice, but the real pacifist is by no means a coward and often needs to be remarkably courageous. Pacifists may believe that nothing is worth fighting for, but that is not the same as believing that nothing is worth dying for. Over the centuries, many of them have suffered and died for their convictions. The truth is that they will die for one principle, and non-pacifists for another. In following their respective convictions, courage will belong to both.

I am not a pacifist. I believe there are evils and tyrannies that should be fought if they threaten my country and her freedom. I believe that Britain embodies values of liberty that I should defend, to the death if necessary. Along with millions of others in Britain and elsewhere, I fought in the last war for these reasons, believing then and now that I was right to do so. I cannot be a non-combatant in life, submitting always to the will of others, no matter how great the evil or how strong the danger to myself and to others. If there is no alternative, I am prepared to fight.

This attitude has been shared by most people throughout history. It is still shared by the great majority of people in Britain today. That does not make it right, but it is the reality. It is incompatible with pacifism and is the point of departure for many of the succeeding arguments over weapons and warfare. A belief in self-defence does not vindicate present defence policy, but it is the premise on which the logic of that policy is based. From it flows the belief that the first duty of a British Government is to defend the integrity and independence of this country. Without security, we have nothing.

The next stage in the logic requires an assessment of the threat that is currently posed to Britain. The preparedness to defend oneself only justifies an actual defence if there is an actual threat. My opinion is that such a threat exists in both a general and a specific sense.

The general threat is ever-present. The experience of history is that the world is never free of aggression and has never known a prolonged period of time in which it has failed to manifest itself. The danger has ebbed and flowed in degree, but it has always existed. One can never predict exactly when it will materialise, as the Falklands conflict illustrates only too well. Such events are the justification for a permanent defence policy. Defence cannot be switched on and off. Its level needs to be adjusted all the time, but its existence is imperative. England has not been invaded for nine centuries, and throughout that time we have maintained strong defences. It would take a brave person to say that, without them, we would have remained a sovereign, independent nation.

To some extent the maintenance of a permanent defence is like insuring one's house against fire: the need for it may only arise once in a lifetime, but the premium has to be paid every year. However, there is an important difference as well. An insurance policy makes no tangible difference to the likelihood of fire occurring, whereas a defence policy acts as a positive deterrent to aggression. In insurance, ninety-nine premiums out of a hundred may be entirely wasted: in defence, no premium is ever wasted, even though one can never measure the precise benefit.

In my opinion, the experience of our history is a sufficient justification of the need for a permanent defence. But the level of our defence capability must depend on circumstances and must be geared to the specific threat that is perceived at the time. When Churchill stood alone in the 1930s, calling for major rearmament, Britain was far from undefended. His argument, tragically vindicated shortly afterwards, was that the defence was no longer commensurate with the threat that was posed, in that case by Nazi Germany. Today, the debate about the required level of defence revolves almost entirely around the degree to which one perceives the Soviet Union as a direct threat to the West. I believe that the threat is indeed real: an opinion that should be explained.

I will start by acknowledging the mistake of viewing Russia's military machine only in terms of aggression. No one should forget, least of all in Europe, that in the last two centuries millions of Russians have lost their lives in wars that were not of their own making. France once and Germany twice have invaded Soviet territory and brought enormous hardship on her people. It is not surprising that Russia should view Europe with the gravest suspicion, should remain sceptical about our reformed character and should make as certain as possible that such invasions never afflict her again. I therefore believe that the Kremlin is genuinely afraid of Western military strength. There is no doubt that much of its rhetoric about Western imperialism is propaganda, aimed at securing the submission of its own people, winning over non-aligned nations, and dividing the United States from her allies, but it also reflects a fear that the West might be tempted to attack the Soviet Union. However, even if one acknowledges these points, it does not mean that Russia is free from all expansionist ambition.

As practised by the Soviet Union, Marxism is an aggressive doctrine, which specifically seeks and envisages world domination. However, many people in the West believe that, while this may be the theory, in practice Russia has given up the intent to pursue it. Yet all the available evidence points to the precise opposite.

It is true that Russia has never attacked a Western nation, but I maintain that the reason for this is the deterrent effect of the West's defences. The Soviet leaders are not fools and they do not embark on projects that carry either a high degree of danger or the likelihood of outrage in the non-aligned world. They are therefore stymied from looking west to Europe and the United States or south-east to China, which they fear equally. But wherever, elsewhere in the world, an opportunity arises for them to intervene in the destabilisation of a country, they never hesitate to take it.

Since the war, we have witnessed in East Germany, in Hungary, in Czechoslovakia and, less brutally but with the same effect, in Poland, the determination of the Soviet Union to impose her will on her East European satellites. After forty years, the Kremlin remains as terrified of the popular will in these countries – and in its own – as ever. And it by no means stops in Eastern Europe. Throughout the rest of the world – in Asia, Africa, Central America, the Middle East and the Caribbean – the Soviet Union has continually fomented unrest, sought to establish Marxist dictatorships and supported these attempts with arms and money.

The view has arisen that none of this amounts to very much. Soviet aggression in Eastern Europe may be 'regretted', but it is semi-condoned on the grounds that these countries almost 'belong' to Russia. Elsewhere in the world, unrest is seen as 'endemic'; after all, 'the Russians are not actually doing the fighting themselves'; in any case, there is 'widespread injustice that needs to be remedied'; besides which, 'the Americans are just as bad'. It has therefore become fashionable amongst certain people in Western Europe to equate the United States with the Soviet Union, to regard them as equally deplorable and to sit with an assumed superiority in the middle.

Throughout this book I attack the notion of only ever looking at one side of a problem and of seeing everything in black and white. But it is equally indefensible to adopt an automatic position at the mid-point between each pair of extremes, and for much the same reason. We all possess, and education is supposed to develop, a critical faculty. This faculty should enable us to see situations from different points of view and not to be purely subjective about them, and it should also enable us to weigh up the evidence and reach a balanced conclusion. Balanced conclusions are not produced by giving equal weight to everything, but by weighing each factor against one's best objective judgment and then deciding where the overall balance lies. A permanent mid-point view is therefore not balanced, because it is just as uncritical as an extreme view. It is intellectually dishonest. There may be occasions when one's judgment says it is six of one and half-a-dozen of the other, but there are many others when the dozen splits far less evenly. In my opinion, the relative merits of American and Soviet foreign policy is emphatically one such case.

We should never forget the contrast between America and Russia themselves, which is important both in its own right and as a reasonable indicator of their respective intentions towards other countries. America is a democratic country that permits freedom of opinion, speech, movement and, as far as possible, action. Russia has a totalitarian régime that represses freedom of opinion, speech, movement and action and feeds its people on a diet of distortions, in stark contrast to the free media of the West. Dissent is not only forbidden, it is rigorously suppressed. Only the state's point of view is allowed to exist. It is disturbing that I should need to spell out these self-evident differences. How is it possible to delude oneself that it would not make much difference under which system one lived? The rebels of the West, who so relish using their freedom to attack the West, are the very people who in the Soviet Union would be in prisons, labour camps, psychiatric wards or unmarked graves.

The difference between the respective sets of allies is equally marked. The Warsaw Pact is a collection of Soviet satellites, compelled by armed force and puppet régimes to submit to the Soviet line. NATO is a voluntary alliance of democratic countries. It is not compulsory to belong to NATO. In this country, the

Labour Party is free to discuss withdrawal from NATO and, if elected on such a platform, would be free to implement it, however catastrophic the result. What does anyone think would happen if Poland tried to secede from the Warsaw Pact? Since its inception, no country has voluntarily joined the Warsaw Pact, whereas every NATO member is a volunteer. And, for those who think that Russian military intervention in Eastern Europe is neither here nor there, I must assume that they would take a similar attitude if America invaded France or Britain.

Turning to the wider world, the fact that the Soviet Union seldom uses her own forces in overseas operations is irrelevant to the issue. It would make the reality far more apparent if she did, which is the last thing that the Kremlin wants. The history of the West has made us too inclined to view world conflict in terms of nationalism. There may be some degree of nationalism in Soviet activity, but its heart lies in ideological imperialism or internationalism. To this end, it does not matter if Russian troops are involved, or Cuban troops, or anyone's troops. Indeed, indigenous troops are to be preferred, as conflict can then be portrayed as a popular uprising. It does not matter to the Russians how it is done, as long as their visible involvement is minimised and as long as the result is a totalitarian Marxist state. In the process, many régimes that are unattractive by Western standards are toppled, which is why some impression of humanity is attached to the coups. But they are invariably replaced by régimes that are just as odious if not more so and, moreover, which exclude any future chance of change for the better.

If one contrasts all this with American policy, there is one fundamental distinction. I accept that, in resisting Soviet encroachment, the United States has been obliged to share some dubious company. I accept that, in these murky waters, the morality of means and ends is hard to disentangle and that questionable judgments have been made, most recently in Grenada. I accept that some of the activities of the CIA may have been very distasteful. But the fact remains that America is resolutely committed to the principle of democracy throughout the world, while Russia is resolutely committed to denying it. Soviet strategy is always to feed on genuine grievances in order to establish a Marxist dictatorship that is not concerned with redressing them.

Sometimes the only way to stop this process is to support the régime that caused those grievances, before something better can be established. We should never confuse or equate this practice – however much we may dislike it – with the permanent Soviet denial of self-determination in all countries, in all situations, at all times.

For those previously unable to see the existence or the importance of this distinction, the Russian invasion of Afghanistan in 1979 must have come as a rude shock. An independent country, with no aggressive intent and not part of the Soviet bloc, was attacked and subjugated by the Russian army. In Afghanistan, the Russians did openly what they do surreptitiously all the time in other countries. For once, they miscalculated the effect on the rest of the world. This event did more to convince non-aligned countries – and many people in the West – of the true threat of Marxist imperialism than anything else. It may be scant comfort to the Afghans, but at least some good has accrued.

For all these reasons I consider the Soviet Union to pose a direct threat to the West. To put it at its mildest, no responsible Government can afford to assume that she does not pose such a threat. I do not want to overstate the danger. I do not believe we are in imminent peril of attack. I do not see reds under every bed. I do not believe that, even if we abandoned our defences, we would necessarily be attacked. But nor do I dismiss the possibility. Even today, the Soviet Union seeks to extend her ideology wherever she thinks it is safe and easy to do so. That is why I am convinced of the need to make it unsafe and difficult to do. That is why I believe that our defence capability should primarily be related to the Soviet military threat, not only in the NATO area, but throughout the world, where the West may ultimately be more vulnerable. In fact, it is imperative that NATO should give more urgent priority to an analysis of the worldwide risks and a strategy for the containment of each threat. A narrow preoccupation with Europe is dangerous.

Some of those who broadly agree with this view would still argue that there is no need for Britain to have more than a minimal defence and that we should rely on the protection of America. It is true, of course, that no country in Western Europe is big enough to defend herself adequately against the Soviet

Union on her own. That is why NATO exists. But the dangers of relying exclusively on America – or on anyone else – would be considerable.

The logic of defence is based on the premise that the British Government has an overriding duty to defend the integrity and independence of this country. If we mortgage our entire security to another country, we are no longer independent. We would be extremely foolish to assume that, under all circumstances and for all time, America will be prepared to come to the rescue of Europe. Why should she? And what right have we to expect it, especially if we are not prepared to make any effort ourselves? Of course, any threat to Europe will always be a threat to America, economically as well as strategically. But I can envisage circumstances in which the Americans might conclude that their intervention would pose them an even greater threat. It certainly should not be taken for granted: many Americans already question their current defence commitment to Europe. Nor should the indefinite continuance of the Atlantic Alliance be assumed. I doubt neither its strength nor its mutual necessity at present, but history teaches us to be wary of the permanence of any alliance. In the course of the last two centuries, we have been allies of Russia in the Napoleonic Wars, enemies in the Crimean War, allies again in the First World War, opposed again at the beginning of the Second World War, allies for the rest of that war and antagonists thereafter. The Atlantic Alliance is under no prospective threat, but I would be reluctant to assume its perpetuity. In 1942, Britain and America found themselves side by side with Stalin's Russia against the immediate danger of Hitler's Germany. I can conceive of future situations where Russia, Europe and America might make common cause against a greater external danger. If that could happen, then so could almost anything.

This leads me to the view that Britain cannot afford to abandon her own defence capability. I accept, of course, that we will continue to be largely dependent on America and our other allies – as they are upon us. We are right to consider the strategic needs of the West as a whole and to provide for them through NATO. But we must also retain a British defence capability within NATO, to whatever extent we reasonably can, and not become dependent on others for everything. In this situation, how do we go about defending ourselves against the perceived threat?

Whatever else may be said of it, defence is a very specific subject. It involves measuring as precisely as possible the capability of the Warsaw Pact countries and assessing what is necessary to resist it. It involves knowing the strengths and weaknesses of their armies, navies, air forces and missiles. It involves assessing the different ways in which they might mount an attack and what we would require to repel each of them. That does not stop fierce arguments amongst military strategists, but the arguments are always to do with practicalities.

In this nuclear age, we have become rather blasé about conventional weapons and their destructive power. This is a dangerous trap and we should remember that the devastation of two world wars was caused, excepting Hiroshima and Nagasaki, entirely by non-nuclear weapons. The chances of a Soviet conventional attack on Western Europe are probably greater than the chances of a nuclear attack. That is why Western conventional defences are of such great importance. They would enable NATO to respond at an appropriate level to a conventional attack and to keep the 'nuclear threshold' as high as possible.

Over recent years, a number of experts have alerted people in the West to the inadequacy of our conventional defences and, to a large extent, I agree with them. NATO is outnumbered by the Warsaw Pact on conventional weapons by about 3:1, and that imbalance has become one of NATO's most pressing priorities. In my opinion, our conventional capability is at its bare minimum and is lower than it should be. The main reason for the imbalance is that conventional weapons and the accompanying manpower are extremely expensive. Nuclear weapons absorb a small proportion of defence expenditure by comparison – less than five per cent. Conventional weapons are expensive individually (a new warship now costs over £100 million) and are required in large numbers to contain the Warsaw Pact armoury. This presents much less of a problem for the Soviet Union than for the West. The Kremlin can spend huge sums of money on armaments without being accountable to its own people. Western defence budgets are high enough anyway, but they are considerably lower, relatively speaking, than that of the Soviet Union and there is little chance of them being increased substantially because of the pressure of public opinion and the other claims on Government spending.

In these conditions, I believe there are two things that the West needs to do. First, we have to state and restate the facts, tell people calmly and rationally what the situation is, and win their support for a sustained increase in defence expenditure while the current imbalance in conventional armaments remains. Second, we need to find more cost-effective ways of providing the equipment. At the moment, despite many years of trying and an array of bureaucratic arrangements established for the purpose, NATO does not make the best use of its collective resources or take full advantage of potential economies of scale. The aim should be to provide a greater capability for the same cost through increased co-operation. This is an aim which I advocated when I was Secretary of State for Defence. Much more effort needs to be put into it now. The initial requirement is for the Governments of all member countries to agree to examine and to rationalise NATO's resources, while making far better use of our technology.

It is argued by some that the obvious solution to the cash constraints on conventional weapons would be to spend less, or nothing at all, on nuclear weapons. I do not agree. My defence of the moral argument for nuclear weapons is made in a later chapter. Here, I want to answer the practical criticisms of current defence policy.

Just as with conventional weapons, there is the need for a nuclear defence that is commensurate with the threat. Defence consists of having a cohcrent protection against all the armaments that may be deployed against one. As long as the Soviet Union has a nuclear capability, so must the West. However loathsome nuclear weapons are, they have been invented and cannot be uninvented. Now that they exist, the ultimate aim may be to get rid of them, but the immediate aim is to prevent them being used. Unilateral disarmament by the West would not inevitably lead to us being attacked, but it would leave the Soviet Union utterly free to blackmail any country in the world on any issue she chose. That is the practical justification for the West's possession of nuclear weapons. It is founded on the belief that the use of such weapons by any nation is far less likely if there is a balance of power than if the power is totally one-sided. This belief is supported by the fact that nuclear weapons have not been used since the end of the Second World War and that, despite mounting conflicts elsewhere in the world, there has been peace in Western Europe for forty years, which must be very nearly the longest period of peace it has ever enjoyed. It cannot be proved that the deterrent effect of nuclear weapons has been responsible for this, but it would be rash to assume that it is irrelevant.

That is the overall proposition which I support. Now I want to consider its implications for Britain. To start with, it is necessary to stop thinking of the collective term 'nuclear weapons' and to understand its component parts. There are essentially three different types of nuclear weapon, on a decreasing scale of destructive power, but each necessary for the maintenance of an effective deterrent.

Strategic weapons are long-range weapons, capable of reaching Russia from America and vice versa. They are much the most powerful and devastating type. The great majority of them are concentrated in (and on) the USA and the Soviet Union. However, two European countries – Britain and France – also possess their own strategic weapons, which is what is meant by 'the independent deterrent'. In Britain's case, the current weapon system is Polaris and the planned replacement for it is Trident.

Intermediate weapons have a shorter range and are capable only of reaching the Eastern Bloc from Western Europe and vice versa. Previously, the Soviet intermediate system was based on SS4 and 5 missiles and the Western system on Vulcan and F111 bombers. Both these systems have become obsolete. Russia then developed a new weapon system based on the SS20 missiles, which are now being deployed. The West has responded by developing Cruise and Pershing II missiles.

Tactical weapons are nuclear warheads fitted to battlefield weapons. They are a development of conventional battlefield weapons, though their use in hostilities would clearly signal a major escalation.

In a general sense, Britain is concerned – like every other country – with the total level of nuclear weapons in the world. But in the specific context of British nuclear defence policy, there are only two real issues. Should we allow intermediate weapons to be stationed in Britain (yes or no to Cruise)? Should we have an independent nuclear deterrent and what should it be (Trident, Polaris or neither)? These two issues are quite separate, unless one is a unilateralist, and they must be discussed separately, although they belong to the same overall strategy.

First, I want to consider the justification for Cruise missiles. Until recently, the intermediate weapons of both sides were obsolescent. They could have stayed that way. But Russia decided to develop a new intermediate system, the SS20s, despite – or because of – the fact that no comparable system existed in the West. She then deployed the SS20s throughout European Russia, trained on Western Europe and also on the Far East. The West had to respond to this new situation for one reason only. However much we are committed to keeping the peace, we have to contemplate the possibility of war. In such a situation, NATO's strategy of flexible response would require the ability to react at an appropriate level to any attack. This strategy was seriously undermined by the deployment of SS20s, to which the West then had no effective answer. A failure by NATO to respond by modernising its own intermediate weapons could only tempt the Russians to suppose that they could threaten Western Europe with their own intermediate weapons, without provoking a response.

That is why the decision was taken to deploy Cruise and Pershing II missiles: so there would be a balanced response, if needed, to the SS20s. Because they are intermediate weapons, they have to be stationed in Europe. The decision to deploy them was a collective NATO decision, by which it was agreed that several European countries would supply the sites and that America would provide the weapons. The British Government agreed that some should be stationed in Britain because it could see no justification for ducking all responsibility for a weapon system that is designed to protect us and the rest of Western Europe.

There was genuine reluctance on our part to deploy Cruise missiles. The decision was taken in principle in December 1979, after lengthy discussions in NATO involving both Labour and Conservative Governments. The West gave four years' notice of the deployment of Cruise and Pershing, and linked the eventual decision with arms control talks. If there was solid progress in those talks, the decision to deploy could be reviewed. Inherent in this so-called 'dual-track' decision was the clear implication that NATO would not deploy the missiles if the Russians withdrew all their SS20s. Instead of withdrawing them, they have increased the numbers week by week over the entire four-year period. Even when all the Cruise and Pershing missiles are deployed, Russia will still have about twice the number of intermediate warheads. To have failed to deploy Cruise or Pershing in these circumstances would have left us vulnerable to an unthinkable extent.

The Polaris/Trident issue is different, and it is confusing and coincidental that it has arisen at the same time. I would defend Britain's continued possession of an independent deterrent on three grounds. First, for the reasons that I stated earlier, it would be dangerous if Britain's defences were wholly dependent on the United States. That argument holds good for nuclear as well as for conventional defences. Second, the fact that Britain and France have independent deterrents affects the perspective of the Kremlin leaders. It is another factor for them to take into account when they consider the West. It gives less point to their strategy of trying to isolate Europe from America. Third, connected with this, it gives Britain in particular and the West in general a better bargaining position in negotiations with the Soviet Union. For all these reasons, we need to have an independent nuclear capability.

If we are to have one, it must be effective. The most futile thing of all would be to waste money on an inadequate weapon and to delude ourselves that it offered us protection. We will never remotely match the nuclear capability of the Soviet Union, nor do we want to, but that does not mean that we cannot have an effective weapon that acts as a genuine deterrent.

Polaris is some twenty years old. It is still fully effective, but it will become obsolete eventually. No one can say precisely when, but it is almost certain to be before the end of the century. New weapons take time to develop and build. Trident will not be completed for another decade. It is the Government's contention, which I endorse, that unless we commit ourselves to a new weapon system now, there is a substantial risk that our current one will be redundant before a replacement is ready. Not only will Polaris itself become outdated, but the submarines which carry it will become outdated too. In the present state of world affairs, it is impossible to justify taking a decision in the early 1980s to dispense with an effective deterrent in the 1990s and beyond, on the assumption that by then the world will be a safer place. That fact cannot possibly be assumed, and is itself dependent on the maintenance of a deterrent.

These are the grounds on which, as Secretary of State for Defence, I sought the agreement of my colleagues in the Cabinet in taking the decisions on Cruise and Trident. In both cases the decisions relate to the fundamental logic of British defence: that we must be protected, that the protection must be commensurate with the threat at all levels, that we must approach the issue within a total Western context, but that we must retain some independence in doing so. I believe that both decisions were not only justifiable, but essential to our security.

So, to return to the earlier question, is the fact that the current level of armaments looks like the product of the madhouse due to a false premise, false logic or some other factor?

I do not believe that the premise is false, nor can anyone who accepts that self-defence is justified. I do not believe that the logic is false: it is only too remorselessly accurate. But I do think there is another factor. It is not enough to think only of the logic of defence, because defence is not an aim in its own right. The aim of defence is security. Defence is one vital part of security, but it is not the only part. Equally important to security is the need to reduce the factors that threaten it in the first place. It is the absence of that fundamental part of the strategy that has produced so much unease in the last few years. Disarmament and defence must go hand in hand. In the nuclear age, neither can bring security on its own.

In my view, there are four options in descending order of desirability: first, a world without nuclear weapons; second, a world where the two super-powers and their respective allies have nuclear parity, which is either static or – preferably – decreasing; third, a world where parity exists, but at an ever-increasing level; fourth, a world where one side disarms, leaving the other with either a nuclear monopoly or clear nuclear superiority.

The crucial point to recognise is that the third stage predisposes people towards the fourth stage, whereas the second predisposes them towards the first. Over the last few years, the reality has slipped from the second stage to the third. In doing so, it has driven many people in the West towards unilateralism, which is the fourth and, in my view, infinitely most dangerous stage. The urgent need now is to halt the third stage where it is and then to draw things back gently through the second, hoping, however forlornly at present, that one day we may reach the first stage. While the impetus remains the way it is, it will always attract people towards unilateralism.

I do not think the West has responded very cleverly to the situation in the last few years. However, I place the primary blame for arms escalation on the Soviet Union. The Kremlin's strategy has been simple. For the past decade, the Russians have pursued a massive arms build-up. The introduction of their new intermediate weapons from 1977 onwards coincided with a time of comparative lack of political leadership in the West, most significantly in America. The Russians hoped to gain a head start over the West – and they did – and then to fight a propaganda war to stop the West catching up. This took the usual form of portraying Western leaders as irresponsible warmongers, intent on starting an arms race and with no serious interest in disarmament.

This strategy was aided considerably by the fact that for four years President Reagan and Margaret Thatcher helped to create just the impression that the Russians wanted. They did it for perfectly understandable reasons. They were rightly determined to close the arms gap, and to provide a defence against the SS20s in particular, and wanted to make sure that Moscow understood their determination. In other words, the rhetoric was directed more at the Kremlin than at their own people. I agree entirely with their sentiments, but I disagree with the fact that they were expressed so frequently, so publicly, in such intemperate language and without any countervailing acknowledgement of the need for co-existence and understanding.

The effect of this rhetoric largely contradicted its purpose. Although the Russians must indeed be convinced of the determination of Western leaders, I doubt it was the words that convinced them. In Soviet ears, action speaks louder than words. They are past-masters at rhetoric themselves and know that it does not always match the action. Their eyes would have been firmly fixed on whether the West actually was strengthening its

defences and whether Cruise and Pershing actually were going to
be deployed. The rhetoric was largely incidental to them, but it
had a far deeper effect on the West. It scared many more people
than it reassured, it made them doubt the wisdom and even the
intentions of Western strategy, and it misdirected the blame for
nuclear escalation on to the West where, on this occasion at least,
it certainly did not belong.

The fact is that the period from 1979 to 1983 was particularly
unpropitious for disarmament prospects. This period included
my time both as Defence Secretary and as Foreign Secretary.
There was much that I should have liked to do, but little that
could realistically be attempted. The West, until the deployment
of Cruise and Pershing, was negotiating from a position of
weakness. The East was not seriously interested because it
thought there was a good chance that Western public opinion,
fanned by discreet Soviet propaganda, would prevent the deployment of Cruise and Pershing and thus secure a permanent
Russian superiority in Europe. In other words, Russia called the
West's bluff and came rather too close for comfort to succeeding.
In the meantime, both sides made well-publicised 'initiatives' and
'proposals', none of them very practical, but with an important
difference. Because Western perceptions of President Reagan
became soured by his rhetoric (and to some extent by his action in
other fields of foreign affairs), public opinion in the West tended
to treat American proposals as a charade while regarding Russian
proposals as a serious contribution to peace – no doubt to the
considerable amusement of the Soviet leaders.

Regardless of the rhetoric, much of the protest and questioning
in the West would have happened anyway. It is also doubtful
whether the Russians would ever have allowed the intermediate
arms negotiations to make real progress until Cruise and Pershing were actually deployed, as is evidenced by the fact that they
walked out of the discussions. It would be wrong to blame
Western rhetoric for all the set-backs of recent years. But the
rhetoric reduced East/West communication and contact to an
almost non-existent level. It bedevilled arms negotiations in areas
other than intermediate weapons. Perhaps above all, I feel that it
increased self-doubt within the West, promoted neutralism and
anti-Americanism within Europe and made the West question its

own moral superiority. These are all important objectives of Soviet strategy. No one can say for certain that these things could have been avoided, but one can say that they might have been.

A similar criticism can be made of much of the debate within Britain concerning the arrival of Cruise missiles. It is both wrong and futile to treat all peace campaigners as enemies of the country. It is wrong because most of them are not. They want the same peaceful world as the rest of us and, however mistaken I and others might think them, they sincerely believe that unilateral nuclear disarmament is the best way to achieve this. People do not give up two or three years of their lives to camp outside bases for something they do not strongly believe in. Universally to impugn their motives and their patriotism is just as insulting and inaccurate as when peace campaigners impugn the motives of multi-lateralists. It is also futile because it is counter-productive. The more that defence becomes an emotional debate on both sides, the more it will favour the unilateralists for the perfectly good reason that all our emotions rebel against the existence of nuclear weapons. The counterbalance to this emotion is a compelling rational argument against unilateralism. The emotion will not go away and nor should it: we must continue to believe in the evil of these weapons. But the logic cannot afford to go away either. Head and heart must march together. That balance can only be struck if the logic is argued calmly, rationally, generously and constantly.

Anyway, whatever the arguments, Cruise missiles are now stationed in Britain and Pershing II in West Germany. Everyone in Europe is more secure, even if they do not feel so. It is true that, although there is a broad parity of strategic weapons, the Warsaw Pact still outnumbers NATO in conventional and intermediate weapons, but that is not as alarming as it sounds. The West's objective is not to match Russia weapon for weapon, but to ensure that our defences are sufficient to act as an effective deterrent and, if necessary, sufficient to repel an actual attack. Because of the action taken in the last few years, I think they now are, except perhaps where conventional weapons are concerned.

I must restate that the substance of Western defence policy over the last four or five years has been correct. I concur with the action taken by President Reagan and Margaret Thatcher and other European leaders, amongst whom Helmut Schmidt and Helmut Kohl should specifically be praised. I am relieved that a crisis in Western defence was met by resolute and courageous political leadership. But the public presentation of the policy was at times clumsy and the paucity of dialogue was harmful. There was no reason why the leaders of the two sides could not have talked to each other, even when there was little immediate chance of progress. Such talks would have maintained a dialogue and increased understanding. They would have made it easier for serious discussions to be resumed when the time came. They would have enabled Western leaders to make their tough statements face to face and in private, which is where they should have been made, and not through the public megaphone. The failure to act in this way not only did damage at the time but, now that our defences have been rebuilt, the new situation has required a volte-face in Western rhetoric, which appears both insincere and inconsistent. In fact it is neither, but the presentation has made it seem that way.

Disarmament negotiations can and must now take place on all levels of weaponry. Even if the Russians are unlikely to make any commitments until the American Presidential election is over and the new Soviet leadership has settled in, there is no reason why the level of dialogue should not be increased. The onus must shift from the exclusive preoccupation with defence to the need for a wider security. In so doing, seven considerations should govern the approach of Western leaders.

First, we must accept that, whatever our views of the Soviet Union, we all need to live at peace in the same world. Co-existence is a practical necessity and cannot afford to be obscured by ideology.

Second, we must remember that our military objective is to have an adequate defence at all levels of weaponry. In some areas this may require parity, but not necessarily in all areas. We cannot negotiate from a position of weakness, but if both sides insist on negotiating only from numerical strength, no talks will ever take place and the arms build-up will continue.

Third, we must recognise that, while a basic distrust will always exist on both sides (and I would say, from the West's point of view, that it is well founded) it is higher now than it needs to be and will only be eroded by sustained personal contact. We must talk to each other. I tried to persuade the Prime Minister that Britain should rebuild a dialogue with the Soviet Union. After President Brezhnev's death, I tried to persuade the Americans that President Reagan should seek an early meeting with his successor. Margaret Thatcher's attendance at President Andropov's funeral represents a change of heart which I welcome unreservedly. However, while top-level contacts are necessary, they are not sufficient. A short summit meeting, where everyone is surrounded by hundreds of diplomats, henchmen, interpreters and microphones, is no substitute for permanent contact at all levels of Government and, indeed, in non-political fields as well. This is how understanding and trust can be built. There are times when it will be difficult to bring about – the invasion of Afghanistan and the shooting down of the Korean airliner, for example, inevitably made contact and communication almost impossible – but it remains vital at all times, perhaps especially at times of difficulty. It is not something to be switched on and off, to be used only when one side thinks it can gain something from the other. It is not a stage show for world publicity. In a patient, painstaking way, it is a continuous necessity.

Fourth, we must stop regarding arms reduction as the be-all and end-all of the process. Of course it remains the objective, but it is not the only thing to talk about and, when progress on arms reduction is unattainable, progress in other areas may still be possible. At the moment, for instance, it is vital for us to discuss verification techniques. There is no point in agreeing arms reduction if either side lacks confidence in the means of verifying it.

Fifth, we must try to look at the world from the Russian point of view as well as from our own. If we did so, I think we would come closer to seeing both the nature of Soviet fears and the constraints on her ambitions. The Kremlin leaders look out of windows that are half Asian, half European, at the uneasy bulwark of Eastern Europe which separates them from the source of previous invasions. They fear the might and power of America beyond. To the south-east, with no buffer but their own defences, they worry about China. They see a wider world that is at best highly dubious about them and at worst openly antagonistic. At the same time, they have dire problems at home. The standard of living is much lower than in the West, and economic inefficiency is widening the gap. Low agricultural production causes severe food shortages. Social problems like drunkenness, truancy and divorce are even greater than in the West. There are severe ethnic problems: before long the Russians will form a minority of the population. Their satellites are a continuing nightmare. All the while, they struggle to impose the Marxist revolution on an unwilling world. All in all, the outlook from Moscow is much bleaker than from any capital in the West. A mixture of fear and ambition drives them to pour huge resources into armaments, which they can ill afford. We need to understand this Soviet perspective on the world.

Sixth, as a result, we should acknowledge that both sides have strong incentives to reduce arms, for reasons both of common sense and of economics. Although each will be wary of the other, we should not view everything that emanates from Moscow as inimical to our own interests. The Russians may wage a propaganda war against the West, while their own régime makes it impossible for the West to influence Soviet public opinion, but we must learn to discriminate between this propaganda and the shared objectives that undoubtedly exist.

Finally, despite all this, let us not be naive. We will not change the Soviet system. We will not quell the driving force of Marxist imperialism. We will not make the Russians devoted converts to liberty and democracy. We will not discover that it has all been a most terrible misunderstanding and that we both believed in the same things all along. Some of these things may happen one day, and let us hope they do, but they will happen as a result of the internal problems of the Soviet Union and not through East–West dialogue. No amount of friendliness or success in arms limitation should tempt us to think that the threat has disappeared. We must not forget how often chronic domestic problems have forced a country's leaders to seek military conquest: Soviet internal problems are as much a threat as they are an opportunity. No Western leader should be deluded into thinking that a generous one-sided gesture on our part will later be reciprocated. The bargaining will be tough and painfully realistic. Warhead for warhead, system for system, the edifice of militarism may perhaps be dismantled. Threats will indeed be reduced in the process – the threat of misunderstanding, the threat of accident, the threat of the sheer volume of armaments – but not the threat of Marxist expansionism. The world would be a safer place, but it would not be secure.

Politicians cannot remove all fears. We can dream of the world as we would like it to be, but we must deal with the world as it is. The reason why fear of war and aggression persists is that it has proved justified on countless occasions in history, in all parts of the world. However, there are some fears that we can eliminate and many that we can reduce, and those are primarily the fears caused by human misunderstanding. Our objective is and must remain to provide the greatest protection we can for Britain and for the rest of the world. I believe that defence and disarmament are two sides of the same coin, which is security. If either is pursued to the exclusion of the other, our overall security is threatened. Both are vital to our well-being. Over recent years, the West has concentrated almost exclusively on defence. There have been some good reasons for this priority, but they are not sufficient to justify the failure to make any serious attempt at dialogue and understanding. The problem is not that we have paid too much attention to defence, but that we have paid too little attention to disarmament.

For every unilateralist in the West, there must be at least another five people asking their Governments to do something positive about arms control. They are right.

FOUR

Britain in Europe

'Great historical transformations are always bought dearly, often after one has already thought that one got them at a bargain price.'
– JAKOB BURCKHARDT

Despite the events of the last forty years, the old love-hate relationship between Britain and the rest of Europe still endures. We have buried our differences as a dog buries bones, always knowing where to find them again should the need arise. The thin stretch of water that divides us from mainland Europe has historically been one of the most significant areas of the globe. Still today, the water confirms a separation, and its narrowness a union that may never quite be consummated. We still speak of 'Britain and Europe', with the ambiguity of the phrase fully intended. We always feel we have the choice of whether to be European or not. It matters to us greatly that we should seem to have that choice, no matter how false it has progressively become.

These tugs from different strings have characterised our attitudes to the Common Market. We did not particularly want to join and now we do not particularly want to leave. We understand that membership brings us benefits we can ill afford to ignore or to lose. We suspect that to withdraw at this point would be damaging. But we have never warmed to the idea of the Common Market, never had any collective enthusiasm for it. We maintain a detached indifference towards it, smiling sadly at its bureaucratic excesses, railing at the chicanery of its other members and liking to claim its successes as British successes and its failures as foreign failures. When British politicians have spoken of the European ideal, we have discreetly averted our gaze from such unseemly outbursts of sentiment.

But beneath the surface run darker emotions. If we were honest, we would admit to a deep envy of the fact that most of our European partners have been considerably more successful than ourselves since the war, in the same way that our latent feeling of patronising anti-Americanism is partly the product of envy. In particular, our pride and our sense of fairness are offended by the prosperity of West Germany. We felt shamed at having to apply for membership of the Common Market in the first place and humiliated at being twice rejected. In different ways, our national pride has been dented time and again in recent decades. No wonder it is liable to erupt in the crude nationalism that makes us take secret pleasure in Common Market show-downs and debacles, no matter what damage is done to the Community and, ultimately, to ourselves. The opinion polls suggest a correlation between these show-downs and the unpopularity of the Community. The more loudly the British Government bangs the table for a better deal, the less popular the Common Market itself becomes. When times are quieter, when the arguments subside, it becomes more popular. This might just mean that, while one part of us instinctively applauds a jingoistic defence of national interests, another part questions whether such a performance is really in our own interests at all.

It is hard to untangle the skein of conflicting emotions and attitudes that condition our response to Europe, but it is necessary to try, or we shall never be at peace with our role. In particular, we need to understand three things: the circumstances in which the Community was founded, how British attitudes towards it have developed over time and the pressures under which the Community itself has increasingly suffered.

We are now inclined to take for granted the fact that European nations are at peace with each other and to forget what a transformation that assumption represents. Not only was physical conflict a recurring feature of Europe through two millennia, but no one regarded the brief intermissions as harbingers of a permanent peace. When conflict was not a reality, it remained an endemic state of mind. These conflicts culminated, in the first half of this century, in the two most devastating wars the world has ever known: confirmation, if any were needed, of the inability of European nations to live at peace with each other. One consequence was the partitioning of Europe, but the other was more positive.

Out of the embers of conflict arose a new spirit of harmony. The strength of this spirit is illustrated by the fact that, not only has there been peace in Western Europe for forty years, but our feelings tell us that this is now a natural and enduring state of affairs. It was this spirit that led to the creation of the European Economic Community. The motive was fear: the need to overcome the aggressive instincts that had prompted the tragedy. The driving force was idealism: the belief that humanity could transform its negativity into a positive assertion of peaceful values. The mechanism was economic: a Community in which member states could work together towards common aims and, in so doing, develop a political affinity as well. Despite the obstacles in its path, the Community has succeeded in its original objectives to such an extent that we now tend to forget the circumstances of its birth.

It is unfortunate that Britain did not join the EEC at the outset. Even if we had joined in the early 1960s, we would have influenced the establishment of the Common Agricultural Policy, the Common Fisheries Policy and the system of financial levies – three areas that have caused us nothing but trouble since we eventually joined. More important still, we would have played a part in shaping the Community's character, and would thus have felt more truly that we belonged to it. After eleven years of membership, we still feel like outsiders. We are only an adopted member of the family. We would like to have been a parent.

It was not that we failed to see a need for the Community, nor that politicians discouraged it. Even during the war, Winston Churchill looked ahead to such an ideal and was as far-sighted about it as anyone else in Europe. We clearly saw a need for the Western Alliance as a whole and were prominent in setting up NATO. But the Community was too big a step for us to take at once, and understandably so.

When Britain emerged from the war, she still ruled the largest Empire the world had ever known. Our eyes were set on a larger canvas than the boundaries of Europe. We saw our role as a world-wide one. Historically, our involvement with Europe was mainly reactive: we intervened only if another European nation sought unnatural hegemony within Europe or was overtly hostile to our interests overseas. We were not greatly concerned with Europe in its own right. Although it was apparent in the aftermath of the war that things would change, it was difficult to foresee how much and how quickly, and almost impossible to foresee what new role we might wish to create for ourselves. We still thought and behaved as the major power we no longer were. In rapid succession, the countries of the Empire were given their independence and the Empire itself became the Commonwealth, with all the adjustments in attitude which that has implied. In the middle of this period, the Suez crisis showed that British independent power was a myth and that the much-vaunted 'special relationship' with the United States was, if not a myth, severely limited in extent.

These were all monumental changes and it is hardly surprising that we did not adjust to them immediately and began to lose confidence in our role in the world. It was only towards the end of the 1950s that we could consider the alternatives in a more positive frame of mind. It was only then that we became serious in our determination to join the Common Market.

Viewed in this context, it is not hard to see that British membership of the Common Market was born out of quite different circumstances to those of the six founding partners. Britain was imbued with the spirit of empire, and to some extent still is. Even when the Empire evaporated, we clung to the hope that we could play an independent role in the world, perhaps in conjunction with the United States. Partnership with Europe was at best our third preference, and this fact has bedevilled our attitude towards the Community, has caused our lukewarm reaction to membership and has bred a natural resentment amongst our partners. Many people in Britain assented to Common Market membership because, economically, they could see others getting richer while we grew relatively poorer and because, politically, they could see nowhere else for us to go. These were not the most positive of motivations. We almost resented the fact that we felt it necessary to join. Idealism was conspicuous by its absence in the country at large; the breadth of vision of men like Ted Heath and Roy Jenkins was scorned more than it was shared.

For all these reasons, British membership of the Common Market did not enjoy an auspicious start. Our scepticism about the European ideal may have prevented us from expecting too much, but it has also encouraged us to measure what we have received in very narrow terms. To make matters worse, the eleven years of British membership have coincided with two developments that have damaged the Community as a whole.

The first is the world recession. The initial fifteen years of the Community, between its foundation and Britain joining, saw a steady upsurge in prosperity throughout Europe and the industrialised world. Everyone benefited, the EEC members more than most. Had we been members then, we would have prospered more than we did anyway and we would have acquired a stronger faith in the advantages of membership. As it is, our membership coincided with the first explosion in oil prices, which depressed growth throughout the West, only to be followed by the second explosion, which triggered the current recession. It is cold comfort to know that the effects would have been much worse if we had not been members of the Community, and we are not inclined to believe it anyway. The recession has made life more difficult for Governments everywhere. When things are going well for everyone, no one inquires too closely whether the very last drop of personal advantage has been squeezed. When things start to go badly, less generous attitudes prevail.

Economic problems have led to the second development, which is the re-emergence of a current of nationalism within member countries, as elsewhere in the world. This should not be overstated: nationalism is still mild compared with its previous eruptions in Europe. Furthermore, the Community should not seek to prevent the sensible pursuit of the national interests of its member states. But some of the signs are worrying, mainly because not enough people are worried by them.

When East–West meetings take place, people hope to hear conciliatory words on both sides. It is our profound wish that a measure of understanding can be reached and that some consensus emerges from the discussions. Should such a meeting break up in dispute and acrimony, only to be portrayed as a triumph for national interests, we would be both angry and alarmed. However, when meetings between Common Market Heads of Government break up in discord, with everyone claiming victory for their own self-interest, we are neither angry nor alarmed, but rather proud. We seem to assume that advantage to ourselves can only accrue at the expense of others. This attitude is by no means confined to Britain. It may run stronger here, but it has become a feature of most countries within the Community.

The reason for this dichotomy is simple. East–West relations are so vital and so fraught with danger to us all, that our fear is great enough to subsume our national sentiments in a wider human concern, as it also was when the Community was founded. But now, European relations are seen as neither vital nor fraught with danger, so the Community provides what appears to be a harmless safety valve for nationalism. That is the extent to which we have forgotten the causes that inspired the creation of the Community in the first place. It is the successful containment of nationalism for the last forty years that now permits us to start indulging it again and to believe this to be harmless. We have come to view harmony as an expedient at times of crisis rather than as a permanent necessity, forgetting that it was precisely this casual attitude to harmony that destroyed it so often in the past.

Unless this tendency is checked, we are on a road of great danger. The manifestation of human nature may change, but its potential does not. The aggression that made Europe a battlefield for centuries still exists and will always exist. We have not abolished it. We are not a superior race of human beings who can afford to deride the follies of our predecessors. We have exactly the same capacity to inflict destruction on each other as we have ever had, and greater means to do it. All that has changed is that we have learnt, from bitter experience, how dangerous our instincts can be. We have not buried our aggression, but have tried to harness it to more positive ends. Instead of believing that we can safely relax this effort in Europe, we should be straining to extend it throughout the world.

It is within this context that I would like to examine the importance of the Community to Britain and the role we should be seeking to play within it. However unfashionable it may be, I will start with the idealism behind the Common Market because, as far as I am concerned, that remains its most vital element.

The Community is based on the principle of partnership, and without that principle it cannot function. Partnership is founded on the simplest of propositions: that the common interest is greater than the sum of individual interests. Each member gives up a degree of independence and self-interest for the good of the whole. Such a principle does not demand that individual self-interest should cease to exist, but that it should not be pursued without consideration to the interests and spirit of the partnership. This represents something more than a temporary alliance, because it is not dependent on a coincidence of self-interest, but on the enduring conviction that the surrender of unbridled self-interest is both desirable in principle and more rewarding in practice.

This is hardly a new concept in human terms, because it has always been the basis of marriage throughout most of the world. Every marriage demands some sacrifice of self-interest by both partners. Every good marriage brings far greater rewards to both partners than either could expect without the sacrifice. Love transforms separateness into unity and alters one's whole perception of self-interest in the process.

I am not such an optimist as to believe that a universal spirit of love and partnership will ever govern the world in practice, but I am not such a cynic as to deride it, nor such a pessimist as to believe that mankind cannot get rather closer to the ideal than it has yet succeeded in doing. Above all, year by year, it becomes more necessary to try. The risks are now greater than ever before, not just because of nuclear weapons, but because of the global ramifications of every small dispute. If rampant self-interest governs the nations and peoples of the world, the consequence will be a catastrophe of one sort or another. That is why we must urgently desist from the unlimited pursuit of self-interest.

Europe is not a bad starting-point for such a process. More than any other peoples in the world, Europeans should – and I think do – appreciate the need for it. We already have a great amount in common through our shared culture, experience and religion, on which we can build in the future. The best features of European civilisation – democracy, freedom, tolerance, respect for the individual and breadth of vision – are precisely the qualities we need to develop and which are conspicuously absent in many other parts of the world. In that case, it is not unreasonable to ask whom we expect to set an example and to give a lead in this respect, should Europe fail to do so. Upon whom falls the mantle of upholding civilised values?

It is in this sense that I am an idealist for Europe. I believe firmly in the spirit of partnership. I think there is a great need for it in the world at large. I am convinced that Europe has to take a moral lead in providing it, and that Britain must be a part of this process. Not only is it impossible for us to fulfil such a role on our own, it is a contradiction in terms: we cannot preach partnership for everyone but ourselves. We need first to show that we can submit to its imperatives and emerge the stronger for doing so.

Just as there is a political necessity for such an approach, there is an economic necessity too. The economic counterpart of self-interested nationalism is self-interested protectionism and it is equally dangerous and misguided. We have learnt through the study of our environment how every species of living thing is interdependent. We are learning through the realities of the world that the safety of each nation is interdependent. We have yet to accept fully that the economic well-being of each country is also interdependent.

Despite its broader opportunities and ideals, the European Economic Community is what its name states – an economic community. It reflects the principle that the interests of its member states are complementary. In my view, that is indeed the reality. Each member of the EEC, including Britain, has bene-fited from it economically, not at the expense of the others, but by working together towards shared objectives. We are not all equally good at producing the same things. Through the Com-munity, we are each able to concentrate on our respective strengths and to have ready markets for what we produce. Britain is a trading nation. Europe is not only our largest available market, but our closest. In eleven years of membership the share of our exports that has gone to Common Market countries has increased by more than a third and the opportunity exists for it to grow still further.

Economically, politically and idealistically the Community is important to Britain and should be seen as such. I can understand the negativity with which we approached membership, but that does not mean that we should remain blinded to its positive values. Nor am I decrying our imperial past, but merely stating the objective facts that the world has changed, the needs of the world have changed and Britain's role in helping to meet those needs has changed. European nations have a vast contribution to make to the future, but they can only do so if they act in unison. I am therefore most concerned about the divisions within the Community at the moment. I do not deny that the problems are substantial, that they need to be addressed and that differences of opinion about the solutions should be aired. But the atmosphere in which these issues are being approached does not help towards their solution. There are three immediate problems and they all relate to the Community Budget:

- far too much of the Budget is spent on agriculture, at present about two-thirds, so there is insufficient money to spend on other important projects, such as regional policy and the relief of unemployment within the Community;

- agricultural subsidies are open-ended, which means both that the overall Budget cannot be controlled and that there is no disincentive to production surpluses;

- there is no consensus on how the Budget should be funded between individual member countries and, specifically, Britain believes that the current system is loaded against her.

At the time of writing, there is a general acknowledgement that these are the immediate problems, but no common view as to how they should be tackled. Although the situation may alter at any moment, I doubt whether all the issues will be resolved for some time, so I will risk outlining the general approach I favour. My view is that, although the Budget is the most apparent problem, the starting-point for reform should be the Common Agricultural Policy. The reduction of agricultural subsidies and the imposition of top limits to them seem almost certain to have three consequential effects. First, such a step would reduce production surpluses and would ideally make the infamous wine lakes and butter mountains a thing of the past. Second, it would reduce the share of the total Budget taken by agriculture and would thus make more funds available for industry and other areas, without requiring an increase in the total Budget. Third, it would also have the effect of reducing the net British contribution, which arises largely because, with our efficient but small agricultural sector, we lose far more than we gain from the steeply rising costs of the CAP. If the overall balance between agriculture and other Community programmes shifted, it would make our financial burden lighter.

This would suit Britain very well, and I believe that it would be better in the long run for the Community as a whole. Also, if there was a parallel reduction of American agricultural subsidies, the farce of a trans-Atlantic trade war at sub-production-cost prices would be stopped, to the benefit of the many countries in the world that now suffer from it. However, such a solution would create severe short term problems for other Community members, notably those that benefit most from agricultural subsidies. It is a fact of life that a Government can more easily refuse a new subsidy than remove an existing one. However inefficient the status quo, it always attracts powerful interests that view its benefits as a right and a necessity. This problem is made more difficult by the economic climate in Western Europe, which gives Governments less flexibility in using domestic subsidies gradually to replace Community subsidies.

However, these difficulties do not alter the fact that a solution must be found – and, in this case, found quickly, which should concentrate the minds of all involved. Because of the open-ended agricultural subsidies, expenditure is now exceeding income, which means that the Community will go bankrupt unless its income is increased or its expenditure reduced. I think Britain has been right to resist suggestions of a short term compromise that patches up the problems on the surface, but makes them ultimately more intractable. The problems go to the very heart of the Community and its objectives. Unless the foundations are right, the difficulties of recent years will continue. They have already caused great damage to the Community and could cause further damage in the future, particularly if the Community is enlarged by the membership of Spain and Portugal.

However, in approaching the issue, two clear distinctions must be drawn. First, there is a difference between an insistence on the need for a long term solution and intransigence on the precise form it should take. The former is a shared need for the Community; the latter can easily become bloody-minded self-interest. Second, as in any partnership, the spirit in which an argument takes place matters as much as the fact of one. An argument conducted in a spirit of friendship and respect is preferable to one conducted in a spirit of hostility and contempt. Both these distinctions are vital to the eventual outcome: flexibility, forbearance and a sense of humour will be needed on all sides.

To give a personal flavour to these comments, I would like to recount my own experience in Community negotiations. When I became Foreign Secretary in April 1982, I was immediately entangled, not only in the Falklands War, but in a crucial stage of the bargaining over the British Budget rebate. Britain had stated the rebate she felt was fair and had refused to compromise. The other member countries did not feel that the claimed rebate was justified and had refused point-blank to sanction it. I had to familiarise myself quickly with the complexities of the negotiations, which had already been in progress for six months. I needed to understand all the details and the nuances well enough to handle the negotiations alone, since Foreign Ministers often hold their meetings without officials present. In this case, such a procedure was formidable for me, partly because the argument was labyrinthine in its convolutions, but mainly because my first priority was the conduct of the Falklands War. Nevertheless, I absorbed the details in time to feel confident that I could hold my own round the table.

My first meeting on the Budget rebate took place in Luxemburg on 27 April. The Belgian Foreign Minister, Leo Tindemans, was Chairman of the Council. He held a series of bilateral meetings to discover each country's position and what room there might be for manoeuvre, but found that the rigidities remained. In due course we adjourned for lunch – to the Golf Club, of all places. The discussion ranged widely for some time and then turned to the British rebate. I had expected a mutual trial of strength and it duly materialised. It was clear that the other nine wanted to see how far they could push me. Needless to say, I was not going to be pushed, at least not at this stage of events, and I adhered strictly to the British position. I made the arguments in my own way – quietly, but firmly – and left them with a sense of my determination, but not of utter inflexibility.

This first meeting was my reconnaissance of the terrain over which the Budget rebate was to be fought and – even more important – of the characters sitting round the table, with whom agreement had to be reached. I was able to judge the mood very carefully: not only was there a total impasse, but also a feeling of frustration, which could easily turn into bitterness. The meeting also confirmed the view I had formed when I had first become acquainted with the negotiations: the British position was untenable. It suited us very well of course, but the other nine could not possibly have agreed to it. Nor would I have done so, had I been one of them. And we had adhered to it for too long.

The principle of give-and-take requires a genuine sacrifice, often when one feels least disposed towards it. It is never difficult to take. Nor is it difficult to give, when one sees the need for it or when the going is easy. It is precisely at the times when one is most convinced one is right, and when others are equally convinced they are right, that the spirit of give-and-take has any real meaning or necessity. That becomes the test of a true partnership. In this instance, I felt that my duty was to judge and to fight for the highest level of rebate to which I thought our partners might agree, while avoiding bitterness and recrimination. My advice was at first criticised by the Prime Minister and the Chancellor of the Exchequer, who felt that I was not sticking up for Britain's interests with sufficient vigour. I fully understood their view, but it did not accord with the reality as I perceived it. The ultimate need was to obtain mutual agreement on the best available terms, which we eventually secured. I would say that Britain's interests cannot be measured by the exact number of pounds in a rebate. In my view, the result least in our interests is to have the other nine members of the Community view Britain as a spoilt child who insists on getting her own way at all costs, thus determining them to make life difficult for us in other ways. Nor did it seem wise to alienate our partners at a time when we relied on their support over the Falklands.

The approach to the current negotiations cannot afford to be governed by intransigence. There has to be a strong and imaginative political will to get to grips with the problems and to solve them. There needs to be a consensus on the objectives of the Community and the means by which they should be pursued. The issue has to be approached in a spirit of partnership, with a recognition of the advantage to all in acting together. Despite the difficulties, there is one factor working in the favour of those concerned. Through a rare combination of events, it is likely to be at least three years before any of the leaders of the three main partners – Britain, France and West Germany – has to face re-election in their own country. This gives a breathing space for reform to be considered and implemented. Domestic pressures exist permanently in all countries, but they may never be less pressing than they are now. To fail to take such an opportunity would be tragic.

Britain will need to make some concessions on her ideal position as she approaches reform. There are three specific areas where we should be prepared to compromise. On the first of them we have already done so: although we were opposed to an increase in the Community Budget and believed instead that it should be restructured, we have now accepted a modest increase in the overall Budget, provided our other objectives are broadly achieved. Next, we should accept that changes in agricultural subsidies and production planning ought to be gradual, as sudden changes are disruptive. Thus we should be more concerned with the principle of the reform than with the time-scale in which it takes place. Finally, we should not be too dogmatic on the precise solution to the problem of Britain's Budget contribution. The Community Budget cannot work on the basis of every country re-covering what it contributes every year. There will always be net contributors and net beneficiaries, varying over time. I agree that the British contribution has been too high for too long and that the method of calculation should be reformed, but in this, as in other matters, we should not set our sights too high or we will miss the target altogether.

Agreement on these issues is the immediate priority, but it is not an end in itself. A solution will not mean that we have reached the finishing post, but only that we will have cleared a few more hurdles on the course. There are many more important questions that we will then need to consider. In doing so, the criterion should be the one laid down by Roy Jenkins a few years ago: that the Community ought only to do the things that cannot be done effectively on a national level. That still leaves many possibilities and, without listing all of them, there are two areas that are especially important.

The first concerns the need to establish a truly common market within the Community. At present, the internal market is securely established for manufacturing industries and, in the main, for agriculture. But in some areas, most notably in financial services, national barriers still exist to an unacceptable extent. This especially penalises the British, because of our competitive edge in financial services, which we are now prevented from exploiting. It seems illogical that a West German company is free to try to take over a firm like Eagle Star, while the West German financial market remains closed to other members of the Community. The establishment of a full internal market is a vital objective, and a timetable should be set for its completion.

The second area concerns a common approach to defence and to international affairs. Co-operation in this field has been excellent in recent years and British membership has strengthened the role of the Community as a whole. We have brought a much broader international perspective and experience, which previously only France – and to a lesser extent Holland – could provide. However, the Community's influence should not be exaggerated. It rests on a limited power base, once the armoury of the United States is subtracted. The result is a steady stream of declarations and diplomatic initiatives, which should not be undervalued, but which lack a cutting edge. I would like the Community to work towards a co-ordinated foreign and defence policy that provides for the needs of Europe with less reliance on the United States. I would not want this alliance to replace NATO, but in time I would expect it to transform NATO into a partnership between America and the Community, rather than between America and individual European countries. If this could be achieved, the Community would have far more effective means to pursue its diplomatic objectives. Instead of trying to wield an influence through words alone, it would have solid backing for its pursuit of peace and stability in world affairs. The effect of such a change would be to make the Community an independent and united power block in the world.

It will not be easy to achieve either objective. National traditions are one obstacle to the first, Irish neutrality to the second. Partnerships are never easy and the need for good-humoured perseverance is continuous. The Community is a complex organisation dealing with complex issues, as everyone is only too well aware. In this chapter, I have chosen not to step into the morass of detail, not to spell out the fine print of possible solutions, not even to mention various other reforms that I would like to see implemented. There is no shortage of others to do so. Instead, I feel that the biggest danger in thinking, writing and taking action about the Community is to become so bogged down in the welter of detail that the real issues continue to elude us. So I have tried to concentrate on what I see as the heart of the matter.

The British people have always been sceptical of starry-eyed idealists, and with good reason. I am not in the least bit starry-eyed, but I firmly believe that the ideals implicit in the Community are of the utmost importance to Britain, to Europe and to the world. We may have been the reluctant bride of Europe because other more appealing matches passed us by. But, within the Community, we have found the means to a greater contribution and contentment, if only we realised it. One of the most fiercely independent nations in the world must learn, not to surrender that independence of spirit, but to submerge it in a wider pool and to offer its values to the world at large. Whether we like it or not, each country in the world is intricately connected with every other. We are all interdependent, nourishing and being nourished in our turn. Victory for us does not entail defeat for others, nor the other way round. In learning to share, we all gain a greater victory. Unbridled self-interest would surely damn us all.

The founders of the Common Market showed great vision, courage and determination, as did Ted Heath when he fought for British membership. It is up to the leaders of the Community today to make its ideal of partnership inspire our imagination continuously, to prove that it can work in practice, and to set an example to the world.

FIVE

The Supremacy of Parliament

'Unanimity is almost always an indication of servitude.' – CHARLES
DE REMUSAT

At the start of the 1983 Election campaign, I ventured the opinion
that a landslide would be an undesirable outcome. The remark
caused quite a stir. The Prime Minister expressed horror at such
a statement and soundly rebuked me. She seemed to feel that no
more agreeable thought could be entertained than to win every
seat available. Yet, as this Parliament progresses, every passing
day confirms just how undesirable a landslide is, for the Government. To put it bluntly, I was right.

If this sounds self-congratulatory, let me add that my remark
was highly unoriginal. It was not a product of some unique
insight, nor even an eccentric whim of my own. Disraeli stated
that 'no Government can be long secure without a formidable
Opposition' and history is a testimony to this truth. The reason is
simple. The heart of British democracy lies in the House of
Commons and not in the Government. Governments may dream
of the glories they could achieve if only they were unfettered by
the need to convince the tiresome House of Commons, but when
a landslide makes this dream attainable it usually turns into a
nightmare. It is in fact the need to convince the 'tiresome' House
that gives Governments some hope of glory, or at least of getting
things right.

Respect for the House of Commons is a cornerstone of my
approach to politics. The process started long before I entered
Parliament myself – in fact on 4 June 1940, when I was just
eighteen. My father was Tory MP for Monmouth and I went up to
Westminster for the day. During the afternoon, he found me a
seat under the Gallery in the House of Commons and there I
heard Winston Churchill make perhaps his most famous speech:
'We shall fight on the beaches . . .'

The early years of the war were one of the proudest periods in

Parliament's distinguished history. But, for me at least, that afternoon had a special magic. It was a Parliamentary occasion of the greatest drama and historical importance. The proceedings were not recorded then and, although I believe Churchill did record the speech later, I must be one of the few people alive today who heard it as it was made. That was the start of a fascination with the House of Commons which has lasted to this day.

I am fortunate to have spent much of my time in government in jobs that have involved me closely with the House of Commons – as a Whip under Harold Macmillan and Alec Douglas-Home, as Chief Whip under Ted Heath and as Leader of the House under Margaret Thatcher. These jobs brought many difficulties, as well as much pleasure, but they enhanced my respect for Parliament and my concern that it should continue to play its vital role in our democracy. For me, no book on contemporary politics would be complete without a chapter on Parliament.

The British political system has been under attack since time immemorial, which is one of the healthiest things about it. At present, the five elements that provoke the greatest controversy are the nature of the electoral system, the balance between the party and the individual MP, the way in which Parliament holds the Government to account, the apparently childish nature of some Parliamentary exchanges and the role of the House of Lords. I have strong views on all these subjects but, before expressing them, I should state the most important point of all – that Parliament is the sovereign guardian of the will of the people and that everything else to do with politics ought to flow from that fact.

There is a myth that the Government is the main democratic institution. It is not. In fact, it is not even elected in a direct sense. The House of Commons is the only national democratic institution. From its elected representatives the Government emerges, and to its representatives it returns. The Government has the job of running the country, but only on the sufferance of Parliament. The Government takes executive decisions, but only in accordance with the powers granted by Parliament. It is Parliament that represents the people of Britain.

If Parliament is elected to represent the country as a whole, it follows that individual MPs are elected to represent their constituencies as a whole. They may owe their election to a party ticket but, once in Parliament, their job is to be the permanent voice of all their electors. In that capacity, MPs have four overriding duties. They must respond to the grievances of their constituents and attempt to redress them. They must constantly monitor and challenge the performance of the Government and decide whether or not to give it their support. They must scrutinise specific legislation proposed by the Government and decide whether it should be passed into law. They must contribute to debates on the main issues of the day, since the House is the focus of the nation's opinion and judgment and will. In modern jargon, MPs individually and the House of Commons collectively are the consumer watchdog on all matters affecting the government of the country.

With this in mind, I want to look at the present criticisms of Parliament. The first concerns the electoral system and the question of proportional representation.

Advocates of PR indict the existing system on three counts: that the number of seats won by each party is out of all proportion to the votes cast, that a large body of moderate opinion is under-represented in Parliament and that the system polarises politics and produces Governments elected on a minority vote that lurch alternately from one side of the political spectrum to the other. I would say that these criticisms amount to only one real charge: that Parliament is not properly representative of the people.

The first comment to make in response to this charge is that there is no such thing as an ideal electoral system. We may sometimes envy the systems of other countries; they equally envy ours. Some criticisms of our system are self-evidently true, but if PR was to be introduced in any of its myriad forms, it would produce its own imperfections. That is not an argument against it, but it suggests the need for a more reasoned approach to the subject than the mere assertion of opposing principles. Sometimes the argument tends to remind me of Bertrand Russell's paradox that 'a fanatical belief in democracy makes democratic institutions impossible'.

In my view, an electoral system should ideally satisfy two needs: an accurate reflection of the popular will, and the capacity for firm and effective government. No system of which I am aware permanently satisfies both needs equally. PR does not necessarily produce weak government, but it can tend to do so. The present system does not necessarily produce unrepresentative government, but it can tend to do so.

The major defence of the present system is that, over a very long period of time, it has achieved a reasonable balance between the two needs. By its nature, it has almost invariably produced firm government. But, also by its nature, it has helped to avoid extreme government. When one party strays beyond the accepted bounds of moderation, the pressures of the system bring it back and offer extinction as the alternative. Within this process, the centre parties act as a barometer to the two main parties: when Labour or Conservative drift too far from the centre ground, the barometer rises; when they return, it falls. In this way, although the popular will may not always be reflected in the Government at a particular moment, it tends to be reflected accurately over time.

The advocates of PR would like to promote the barometer, so that it controls the weather rather than reflects it. I do not believe that this would result in Governments with greater popular support than at present, although it would moderate the extremes of opposition and would thus produce Governments that conformed more closely to the popular average. However, it would also tend to produce coalition Governments and, in my opinion, coalitions are often – though not invariably – weak. I also feel that a major constitutional change of this nature should only be made under extreme duress, especially when the present system has stood the test of time so well.

From this it will be gathered that my clear preference is for the existing electoral system. However, that support depends considerably on how the system is operated. If a Government listens to other people and tries to win consent for its policies from the nation at large, I believe the present system provides the best of both worlds. If a Government relies on its Parliamentary majority to railroad extreme measures, the system loses much of its justification. It was my fear of the growing extremism in the Labour Party in the 1970s that caused me to urge the Conservative Party not to close the door on PR. That particular threat has now subsided, but a full return to the politics of consent has yet to occur. I hope and expect that the present system will cause it to do so. If it does not, the pressure for PR will inevitably increase.

The second area of controversy is the balance between the MP as an individual and the MP as a member of a political party. Many people outside Parliament feel that MPs are too subservient to the party line; many Governments feel that some of them are not nearly subservient enough. Both complaints are understandable.

Since almost all MPs are elected because of the party they represent, it is not surprising that party leaders should expect them to be loyal to the party. However, if one pursues that argument to its logical conclusion, every MP would be unfailingly loyal to the party and Parliament would become meaningless. MPs would either cease to form their own judgments or would feel obliged to keep quiet about them. The result of every vote in the House of Commons would be a foregone conclusion. Indeed, it would be pointless to take a vote once the party leaderships had declared their views. The whole thing would be as much a nonsense as the block votes of unions at a TUC Conference. In Parliament, blind loyalty is untenable and uniformity is impossible. Every adult in the country has a personal point of view and it is desirable for the widest range of these views to be represented in Parliament. It is therefore undesirable that all the members of a party should hold identical views. It is both vital and inevitable that there should be a diversity of opinion. Political parties exist to simplify diversity, not to crush it.

Prospective MPs will have chosen a party to support on the basis of their own beliefs, a process that implies some common ground between all members of a party. At an election, candidates will be standing in support of the manifesto put forward by their party and have a duty, in my opinion, to subscribe at least to the main tenets of that programme, to indicate where there are points of difference and subsequently to support that programme in Parliament if their party has the opportunity to enact it as the Government. It is imperative for the electors to know what broad approach and measures each candidate supports and this is indeed the justification for the party system.

It is beyond this point that individual judgment must be exercised. There still remain many areas of debate where no MP should be ashamed to take an independent view. Failure to do so can amount to a dereliction of duty. One cannot draw a finite line between 'moral' issues, on which all views are permissible, and 'political' issues, on which only one view is permissible. Political issues have moral dimensions and vice versa. There is never only one point of view on any matter and the best decisions are reached by debating the alternatives openly.

A sensible party will understand that, with several hundred MPs, there will be a range of views on how to tackle the problems. The party will choose a programme to put before the electorate after a process of consultation amongst its own members and with a sense of what the nation as a whole wants. It will then expect its MPs to give it their broad support. At least nine times out of ten, that will happen naturally, but there will be times when attitudes differ. This occurs frequently with regard to issues of the future, where no firm policy exists. It also tends to occur when a Government is a few years into a term of office. At this point, circumstances may well have changed since the election and policies may need to be adapted. No one should view an election platform as a five-year sentence to static opinions without the option of adjustment. A wise party is neither driven by defensiveness to fear these differences, nor tempted by fanaticism to suppress them.

In this way, the matter ceases to be a simple conflict between party loyalty and individuality. Support for the main elements of an election platform amounts to more than party loyalty: it is loyalty to what one stood for oneself and what one's constituents voted for. On the other hand, dissent does not imply disloyalty to a party, but the expression of a view that one believes is in the interests of the nation, even if a majority of one's colleagues disagree with it at that particular moment.

This is not a late-conceived view to justify my own expressions of limited dissent: it is an opinion I have always held and have practised when it was hardest to do so. My period as Government Chief Whip coincided with several controversial measures dealing with industrial relations, immigration, local government and, most of all, membership of the Common Market. These issues were the subject of heated debate within the Conservative Party, as well as in the country at large. I never stopped anyone from expressing their opinions publicly, although I occasionally tried to dissuade them from doing so when I felt it would be unnecessarily damaging. I took the view that Members were elected precisely in order to state their opinions and that the House was entitled to know what they were. It was up to Ministers to win the argument. All I asked was to be kept informed as to when such opinions were going to be expressed. This did not prevent the Government measures from going through – and it was my job to make sure that they did go through – but it meant that different views were fully aired and that nobody felt aggrieved in the process.

In particular, the handling of the European Communities Bill was a testimony to the value of allowing a full expression of views. There were a number of people in the House, and many more outside, who believed that the Bill would fail. I convinced myself otherwise, and the task of getting it through dominated my life for many months. The principle I followed was that the Whips would remain in close touch with all Members, whatever their views. Quite often I held meetings with the anti-Marketeers, with whom I had the friendliest relationship. There were no hard feelings. They knew what I was going to do and I knew what they were going to do. We were all true to ourselves. So, although this Bill had perhaps as contentious a passage as any in this century, when the struggle was over, everyone felt that the battle had been fully and fairly fought and honour was satisfied.

Apart from recognising the intrinsic merits of independence, this attitude makes life easier for the party and enables its leaders to reach better decisions. If the leadership pays too little heed to the views of its supporters, it can become unimaginative and out of touch. A two-way flow of opinion benefits both sides alike. Besides which, it is ultimately impossible for dissent to be repressed and, if the attempt is made, the eventual eruption will be far more violent and divisive than it need be. Most politicians can accept that their views put them in a minority – some positively relish it, though I am not one of them – but few can accept their views being ignored. Everyone in the House of Commons has an opinion, however foolish one may think it is, and it ought to be expressed and heard. That is why MPs are there.

The delicate balance between the party and the individual has tipped more towards the former in recent years. Two factors have encouraged this process. First, the party machines have attached increasing importance to the precise political views of aspiring candidates. In the Labour Party this trend, combined with the party's constitution, has made many of its MPs and candidates virtual prisoners of sectional interests within the party. I see this as a dangerous and undemocratic process, far removed from the British Parliamentary tradition. The prime tangible consequence of it has been the break-away of the SDP.

The second factor is that MPs have become more career-minded and career-dependent than they were. The previous situation in which many MPs, particularly in the Conservative Party, had demanding jobs outside politics and frequently neither sought nor wanted government office, was derided by many people. However, it did permit and encourage MPs to exercise greater independence of judgment and it also gave them, in many instances, a greater experience of the real world than any full-time politician can acquire. The British amateur tradition became a laughing stock but, now that we perceive the effect of its absence in all walks of life, there is a yearning for the qualities it embodied. It is true that career politicians have always existed, and have depended on patronage from their seniors for advancement. Legitimate ambition is not to be criticised in itself, but when more and more MPs hunger for government office, the pressure to conform can become unhealthy. Most MPs still speak their mind, but increasingly they tend to do so in private whispers and not in public debate. If MPs start looking on their party leaders as employers, the consequence will be that party leaders will increasingly look on them as employees.

The need for a strong sense of individuality is especially great in the modern world. The whole drift of life, the whole march of technology, is tending to diminish scope for the individual. Not only has the state become progressively more powerful, but so has almost every other corporate institution. The tide is almost irresistible at present and, despite Margaret Thatcher's deep dislike of it, has continued to rise under her Government. There has never been a greater need for MPs to remember that they were elected to Parliament not as delegates of a political party, nor of a particular interest group, nor of a specific ideology, but as representatives of the people. Unless MPs retain their own sense of individuality, they will not be able to stand up for independent values in the nation and Parliament will become another piece of apparatus of the corporate state.

This leads to the third controversial issue – the way that Parliament holds the Government to account. There are three means by which the House of Commons can achieve this, other than through votes in the Chamber. The first is by challenging proposed legislation, both in debate and during the Committee Stage of a Bill. Many people may not realise that legislation is often changed considerably during the Committee Stage. Public attention is drawn to the set-piece speeches, which tend to be polemical in nature. In Committee, constructive amendments are frequently made, many of them proposed by the Government as previously unconsidered aspects of the matter emerge in debate. Further amendments often take place in the House of Lords. Indeed, it is a rare event for a Bill to pass through both Houses without amendment. Parliament exists not only to approve or disapprove proposed legislation in principle, but to scrutinise it in detail and to improve it where possible.

The second aspect of Parliamentary control is handled through the system of Select Committees, which was extended a few years ago. I played a leading role in bringing the Conservative Party and Parliament to accept the new system, from 1978 onwards. At that time, I was Shadow Leader of the House, and it was the long and important struggle over devolution of powers to Scotland and Wales that led me to think more deeply about the inadequacies of our Parliamentary procedures at that time. Since 1945, government had increasingly pervaded our everyday lives, but Parliament had not adjusted itself to scrutinise this activity. Although some Select Committees had existed for a long time, there were large gaps in their collective scope. There was a need for a framework of Select Committees that would cover all the Departments and activities of government on a systematic basis, and which had the power to call on witnesses and documents and to publish their findings. After some argument, this proposal was eventually included in the Conservative manifesto in 1979. After the election, the issue came up early to the Cabinet. Needless to say, there was not unanimous support for a system that might have the effect of embarrassing individual Ministers. Whitehall also had reservations about it. Naturally, I was determined to see our commitment honoured, and was supported by most of the Cabinet, and especially by Norman St John Stevas, who was then Leader of the House. The new system was established in November 1979.

I believe it to have been a success. It is fair to say that much of the work of these Committees goes unnoticed by the public. Indeed, most people probably only know of them through the farcical series of leaked documents that peppered the 1983 Election campaign or through the recent controversy over GCHQ. It is inevitable that the controversial reports will receive most attention and that when, as often happens, a Committee expresses satisfaction with the performance of a particular Minister or Department, the media will not report the fact. This is regrettable, but it does not invalidate the system. Already there have been moves to extend the Select Committees. I think this would be a mistake until they have matured for a little longer, although I would like them to be given a stronger back-up staff. It is also vital to safeguard the principle that the Government collectively and its Ministers individually are accountable to the whole House of Commons, and to nobody else.

Both the scrutiny of particular Bills and the monitoring of Government performance through Select Committees are important means by which Parliament can help to improve the quality of government. The third way in which Parliamentary control is maintained is through a vigorous and effective Opposition, which brings me back again to the question of a landslide.

Experience shows that a large Parliamentary majority has an equally harmful effect on both Governments and Oppositions. It encourages Governments to take Parliament for granted. It can make them careless and complacent. It tempts them to take undue risks. It discourages them from listening to their own back-benchers or to the country at large. It makes unity among the governing party harder to achieve. It also tends to demoralise the Opposition and to make them feel there is no point in devoting time to constructive amendment. It promotes violent rhetoric rather than dialogue. It leads Opposition members to look increasingly outside Parliament to make an effect. Parliament becomes weaker and, as a result, Government becomes weaker.

It is essential that the Opposition should expose faults in the Government's performance and flaws in its programme. There is no more effective deterrent to Ministerial complacency or incompetence than the threat of humiliating exposure in the House of Commons. This keeps everyone on their toes and inhibits ill-conceived or ill-considered action. The Opposition is the permanent reflection of the other point of view. But it also needs to construct a positive platform of its own, especially at the time of an election. One of the features of the 1983 election was the failure of the Labour Party to assemble more than a patchwork programme of varying degrees of unpopularity and implausibility.

A constructive Opposition should imply some agreement with the Government on major national objectives. Parliament operates at its best when there is a fierce debate about the means to achieve a common end. One of the problems of the last decade, brought about mainly by the dominance of the left-wing within the Labour Party, has been that there is now almost no agreement on anything between the two sides of the House of Commons. This renders debate virtually meaningless. It has also led to a situation where a change of Government has caused the undoing of much that the previous Government attempted. Whether one regards the doing or undoing as the harmful part depends on one's point of view, but what is certain is that the constant chopping and changing has been detrimental to the country in general and to industry in particular. I am the last person to argue for uniformity, but a certain degree of stability and continuity is essential to good government.

As a postscript to these comments, it would be unfair to leave the impression that the House of Commons is a permanent battleground of entrenched enmity, however much it sounds like it on the radio. On a personal level that is certainly not the case. There are numerous opportunities for MPs of different parties to exchange views and to make friends. On a formal level, the Select Committee procedure helps to bridge the party divisions. Members of these Committees have a sense of representing Parliament, not just their own parties, whereas the fact that some proceedings are in private takes the stridency out of the debate and creates a less polarised environment.

The atmosphere of the House, the way in which debates are

conducted and the general tone of Parliament is another controversial issue. For as long as I can remember, but more particularly since the advent of sound broadcasts, many people have considered the behaviour of MPs during debates to border on the infantile. There are jeers and catcalls, cheers and groans. There appears to be a running sound effect of 'rhubarb, rhubarb'. Is it surprising, people ask, that politicians are held in such low esteem when they disport themselves like this?

My response is that it depends on what sort of Parliament one wants. The House of Commons may be all the things its critics say, but it is also vivacious, human and remarkably unintimidating. Most MPs feel free to vent their feelings openly, which often means noisily. The design of the Chamber has always encouraged confrontation: the Government and Opposition facing each other and arguing across the floor of the House. This has been the nature of the House of Commons for 700 years – or from whenever one wishes to date it – and I believe it makes for the most lively democratic assembly in the world. It has many imperfections, but these are inseparable from its strengths. From my point of view, the imperfections of an alternative style would be far worse, as is evidenced by the assemblies of many other countries. They are arid, clinical and boring. They may have a veneer of greater dignity, but their style is antiseptic and lacks the spontaneity that makes the House of Commons unique. I am not surprised that this impression is not shared by those who listen to the broadcast debates, but then Parliament is not designed for armchair listening, nor should it be. To most of its many members over the centuries its style has seemed admirable because it encourages the expression of human reactions and emotions.

So far I have written about the House of Commons, although several points are equally applicable to the House of Lords. The second chamber is also an issue in its own right. Its value has been questioned for a long time and many reforms proposed, including abolition.

The House of Lords presents something of a dilemma. As long as it remains unelected, its power and effectiveness will be constrained, as its members will not wish to be seen to frustrate the will of an elected House of Commons. On the other hand, if it became wholly or partially elected and thus felt freer to exercise its power, one would have two competitive elected bodies, which could well become enmeshed in permanent conflict if the majority in the Lords was at odds with the majority in the Commons.

Despite the limitations, the House of Lords performs a function that is valuable to the point of being indispensable. The very existence of a second chamber is a necessary check on abuse of power by the first. I think most people in the country have a great deal of respect for the House of Lords and would be totally opposed to its abolition. Many of its members have valuable knowledge and experience to bring to bear on a wide range of issues, which compensates for the fact that by definition there are few young peers. Most legislation is improved by its passage through the Lords. The peers make a very substantial contribution to the political process.

I think that one day the House of Lords will be reformed, and that a broad measure of agreement will emerge as to how it should be accomplished, but it does not exist at the moment. In 1968, there was agreement on reform between the leaders of both main parties, but the combined weight of the back-benches defeated the combined weight of the front-benches. The Opposition featured an unholy alliance between Michael Foot and Enoch Powell and concealed a vast disparity in motive, but it is a good example of the successful use of back-bench independence. The attempt has not been repeated and, although some of the most experienced peers are keen on reform, I do not sense any great enthusiasm for it in the Commons or in the country at present. My own inclination is to leave well alone, at least for the time being. The current composition of the House of Lords may lack any logical justification, but at least it works.

Reform of the House of Lords will undoubtedly remain an issue in the future. In conclusion, I would like to mention some other changes that might improve the performance of Parliament. As my earlier comments imply, I am vehemently opposed to the televising of debates, as I was also opposed to their being broadcast. Opponents of televising are variously criticised as anti-democratic (which I am not), old-fashioned (which I may be) and afraid of what would be revealed (which I am). I am not afraid of the revelation because I am ashamed of the reality, but because I have no confidence that television will portray the reality, any more than radio does, at other than a superficial level. I am not enamoured of the thought of MPs tailoring their Parliamentary performances to a popular audience instead of to the House itself. I expect the change will come, but I believe it will prove to be damaging.

There are, however, three positive changes that I would like to see made. The most substantial is to reduce the number of MPs. Since most MPs would rather see the number increased, as has recently happened, my view has little chance of success. It is a view that has grown out of my experience over two decades and especially in the Whip's Office. My feeling is that it does not take 650 MPs to look after the nation's interests, that such a number is unwieldy to manage, and that Parliament would be more effective if there were fewer MPs. The standing and authority of MPs would also be enhanced. I do not believe this would create constituencies of unmanageable size. Until 1983 my own constituency had 99,000 electors and I cannot say that I found it much harder to attend to than I do now with 68,000 electors. Such a reform may seem unrealistic, but I think it is desirable.

Equally desirable, but more realistic, is a wish for shorter hours. There is an unanswerable argument for late sittings, since the purpose of Parliament is to allow dissent and grievances to be aired, and for members of the Government to be present to receive the brickbats – or even bouquets – from the people's elected representatives. One must be careful not to reduce the scope for legitimate debate. Even so, it is surely reasonable to insist that the House should only sit late into the night if a certain number of MPs – perhaps thirty – positively indicate the desire for it. At the moment, in certain cases, debate can continue all night on the whim of one or two MPs. The antisocial hours put added strain on the marriages of MPs and I doubt if many wives or husbands will go on finding them acceptable.

Connected with this is the question of whether all Bills presented to Parliament should have a timetable for each of their stages and main provisions. The argument against is that the use of delaying tactics is one of the few weapons the Opposition possesses and that it should not be curtailed. The counter-argument is that this right is often curtailed anyway by the Government's use of the guillotine motion and that, since the guillotine is usually employed only after an Opposition attempt to filibuster, the current effect is that some clauses of controversial legislation are debated at inordinate and unconstructive length, while others are scarcely debated at all. I share this view and believe that, with an enforceable timetable, it would be possible both to maintain effective opposition and to devote proper attention to all sections of a Bill. I would certainly like to see the Committee Stage of major Bills organised on this basis, although a corollary of this must be to ensure that the Government is not enabled to increase the number of Bills it introduces. The objective is better scrutiny, not more legislation.

Fewer MPs, shorter hours and a timetable for major Bills are three reforms which I support. I believe they would all help to improve the performance of Parliament without affecting its character. Throughout its long history, our system has always managed to adapt to changing times in a process of continuous evolution, while retaining its distinctive style. The process cannot stop, but it should not be accelerated by ill-considered changes that might upset the fragile balance. The need for efficient Government must be tempered by the need for effective Opposition. The need for party loyalty must be tempered by the need for independent opinion. The effectiveness of Parliament depends on these balances being maintained. Above all, it depends on the good sense and humanity of its members.

For me, the House of Commons is a most marvellous place. It is rich in friendship and rivalry, in good humour and harsh criticism. It can be the kindest place in the world; it can also be bitterly cruel. People can make a great success of their lives there, and then something may go wrong and the House will turn against them. Anything can happen, but it is never less than human. Thanks to the generosity of the electors of Cambridgeshire, it has been my great privilege to be part of it all for over twenty years.

SIX

Morality and Politics

'Neither way is better. Both ways are necessary. It is also necessary
to make a choice between them.' – T. S. ELIOT

If politicians earned a royalty from the jokes told at our expense,
we would all be millionaires. And, if the jokes were true, we would
be the most devious, dishonest, cynical, mendacious, cunning,
insincere bunch of double-dealers ever to walk the earth. On top
of that, we are labelled as self-righteous hypocrites, who compound our other moral felonies by posing as paragons of virtue.
Doubtless this accounts for the whoops of moral indignation,
coupled with gleeful self-satisfaction, that accompany any public
exposure of our private failings.

If this is our image, we have only ourselves to blame. The most
damning indictments of politicians come from the mouths of
other politicians. We are specialists in spotting the motes in the
eyes of others. It has always been thus and probably always will be.
Politics have to do with the acquisition and the use of power. In a
democracy, the pursuit of power is inseparable from the clash of
ideas, and rash statements abound in the war of words that
follows. Individual politicians are worshipped by their supporters
and reviled by their enemies, while their collective reputation
suffers.

This is hardly a new phenomenon, but neither is it unvarying.
In the past, politicians have sometimes been held in far greater
odium and contempt than they are now, difficult though that may
be to imagine. However, at other times they have inspired a large
measure of public trust and respect. I would say that the quarter
century between 1940 and 1964 saw politicians of all parties held
in greater esteem than in the years before or afterwards, although
this may be changing again. A large pinch of scepticism is
healthy, but a grossly unflattering image is not inevitable, nor is
it desirable, nor – in my opinion at least – is it altogether deserved.

Politicians are not angels. We match the mores of the society we represent, and society is not composed of angels. But neither are we greater devils than the world at large. Indeed, we are a mirror of the world, and those who condemn us are often condemning their own reflections. What differentiates us from most other people is that we are engaged in a job that exposes the gamut of personal and collective moral choices under a permanent public microscope and to a constant chorus of criticism from our colleagues. How well would anyone stand up to a battery of critics whose main intent was to expose one's every failing?

I do not wish, even if I were able, to prove that politicians are models of integrity or to rebut their public image. Still less do I wish to lay down universal laws of political behaviour. Moral absolutes exist in theory, but when they meet reality they wear many faces. The crystal remains intact, but it exists as a prism, shedding a different light depending on the angle from which one views it. To condemn a moral viewpoint that differs from one's own as immoral is purely subjective, and thus subject to fallacy. The whole book is an expression of personal opinions, but this topic is more subjective than most. Nevertheless, I want to consider the way in which morality and politics interact and to examine the conflicts that arise, in order to demonstrate the delicacy of the choices that have to be made.

First, however, I want to consider the moral basis of government itself, in terms of both purpose and authority. Many philosophers have pontificated on the moral purpose of government. The definition most often repeated is Bentham's: 'the greatest happiness of the greatest number'. The reason for its repetition is that it is such a bland statement that no one can substantially disagree with it. The questions it raises are rather more significant than the question it answers. What is happiness? Who defines it? Can Governments deliver it? Also, since 'the greatest number' implies the existence of a smaller number, how does one balance the conflicting needs of majorities and minorities? In view of this, one might more modestly substitute the definition: 'to help to match people's opportunities with their desires'. However, this statement is another truism, to which Marxists, moderates and fascists could equally subscribe. The fact is that there is little dispute as to what moral purpose government should ideally fulfil, but every dispute in the world about the means to its fulfilment. The ideal is a platitude, splintered by reality.

The question of the moral authority of government is less vague, as it forces a distinction between democratic and totalitarian régimes. This at least answers the question as to who defines happiness. A democratic Government draws its moral authority from the fact that it has been freely chosen by the people and that its tenure of office is determined by popular consent. A totalitarian government draws its moral authority – for those who think it possesses any, which I do not – from the notion that the state is indivisible from the people and therefore automatically represents their interests.

However, in a democracy, the matter does not end here. Many people, myself included, would say that, even though a Government may have a laudable moral purpose and a general moral authority, it does not thereby have a moral right to do exactly as it pleases for five years. It is with this justification that some union leaders flout current legislation on industrial relations. Here they tread on dangerous ground. Although Parliament's legal authority may not always be synonymous with a moral authority, in practice the two must be treated as the same, or else any person or group in the country could claim immunity from the law by disputing its moral authority. However imperfect, the law is the only objective means of separating right from wrong in practice. Also, in this instance, the Government's platform at two elections, supported by the weight of public opinion and even union opinion, must give its legislation moral as well as legal authority. But I accept that, in principle, there is a distinction between the moral authority of a Government generally and its moral authority for specific legislation, even if it is a distinction that Oppositions frequently confuse and abuse for their own ends. However, the fact of admitting to it in principle means acknowledging that different people will invoke it in different ways in practice. Thus, even in a democracy, the moral authority of government is at least partly subjective.

The more one considers the theory, the more it seems meaningless without the practice; the more one considers the practice, the less straightforward it becomes. An ideal Government policy would harm no one and benefit everyone equally.

That ideal does not exist. It is possible to take action that causes no harm, but its benefits are seldom equal. It is constantly necessary to make choices as to which sector of society one wishes to assist or reward and, sometimes, which sector one wishes to penalise.

This Government's objective is to create a thriving, competitive economy, with efficient companies providing secure employment for the nation. It is the Government's view that this achievement would be jeopardised by propping up unviable businesses and lavishing money on the creation of phony jobs. Therefore, it believes that high unemployment in the short term is an unavoidable price of economic recovery: one group of people has to be penalised now to create ultimate benefits for all. Whatever my views on the implementation of this policy, I can see that it is at least a tenable argument. For anyone who truly believes in the proposition, the policy that follows from it is not just economically correct, but the only moral alternative. This does not vindicate the proposition or the policy, but it means one should pause before attacking them on moral grounds. If one condemns on principle every policy that causes short term hardship, all that remain are short term policies. Once it is accepted that 'perfect' solutions do not very often exist, it follows that a politician's moral view of a problem is bound to match the political or economic assessment that precedes it.

On the surface, this might seem an outrageous claim. We are taught that the moral view should come first and that the practice should follow. An individual will believe it right to be kind to other people and not to harm them, and will then attempt to behave in that way. Why should politicians be allowed to put the practice first and the morals second? In fact, we are not doing so. We start with an abstract principle – wanting to benefit people – proceed to a practical assessment of how best to do so, and then reach a conclusion that unites both. However, this approach does differ from personal morality in two respects.

The first is that, in politics, one seldom deals in certainties. The aim is to benefit people and not to harm them. But, whereas individuals usually know when they have spoken an unkind word or failed to help others, politicians have no equivalent certainty as to which policy will truly serve people best. It becomes a matter of personal conviction as to how the moral purpose is best served, which is why a moral course follows a pragmatic assessment. The second difference between personal and political morality is that, as an individual, one usually has a free choice to accept or reject a particular course of action. Circumstances may modify one's moral attitude, but they seldom prevent one from carrying it out, if one is determined to do so. In politics, no democratic Government has unlimited freedom of action and even totalitarian Governments have sometimes to take account of other views. Some politicians are more disposed to compromise than others, but there has never been a democratic politician who has not been obliged to compromise on some occasions.

Compromise has become a dirty word in politics: it is now fashionable to be uncompromising, although – like most fashions – it will not last long. The fact is that there are good compromises and bad compromises. Every circumstance is different. The principle of compromise is to give up something in order to gain something and the question always is whether the price is justifiable. A refusal to yield is not always strong and a preparedness to give way is not always weak: sometimes it requires a greater moral strength to compromise than it does to stand firm. If compromise is based on an absence of courage or principle it has no merit, but if it is based on the courage to recognise the legitimate principles of others and to find a way of unifying a fundamental discord, it serves a high principle of good government.

One example of the complexities of this issue is the involvement of politics with sport, and in particular the debate on sporting contacts with South Africa. Both sides hold contradictory moral views with equal vehemence.

The first view runs as follows: 'South Africa is a racist state, which denies almost all forms of expression and opportunity to the majority of the population. Any contact with the country gives legitimacy to its régime, endorses its racial policies and diminishes the chance of change taking place. A boycott of South Africa is both morally correct and the best practical assistance the rest of the world can give to force a change in the system.'

The opposing view is this: 'Nothing alters the fact that sport should not be confused with politics. Sport is to do with contact and competition between individuals, and its value is that it brings people together in a world where most other things drive them apart. It is a positive moral wrong to ostracise people with whom one disagrees, and it is through human contact that changes are most likely to be made in the system.'

As so often happens, Christian teaching is invoked on both sides. One side insists that Christ commanded us to fight evil; the other that He instructed us to love our enemies. Most people will recognise their own point of view in one of the above paragraphs and will decisively reject the other. Yet can anyone with an open mind really claim that either view is wholly indefensible? Unless one positively supports the South African régime, I do not think one can.

Like most people in Britain, I broadly support the second proposition. I would have preferred that politics had never been dragged into sport in the first place. But I cannot deny the sincerity of the opposing view and, as a politician, I cannot avoid the fact that sport *has* become embroiled in politics. There is therefore a clear choice to be made. Given that those who hold the opposing view are intractable on the matter, one can either back down or stick with one's principles and take the consequences. In this case, the consequences would include a sporting boycott of Britain by most black countries and the probable collapse of events like the Olympic and Commonwealth Games in the ensuing acrimony. To take this course would have the practical consequence of nullifying the principle on which it is based, because it would deny British sportsmen and women contact with those of other nations and vice versa.

The situation is a paradox. If one fights for the principle of sporting contacts, one will end up losing many of them. If one concedes the principle, one will end up keeping them all, except where South Africa is involved.

I believe that in this instance compromise was the correct course although, whenever there is a total contradiction of principle, an agreement will be more of a capitulation by one side than a compromise by both. The Gleneagles Agreement may be unsatisfactory but, in the opinion of most politicians at least, it is preferable to the alternative. Many people passionately disagree with it, but I wonder if they would still do so after years of an anti-British boycott. At least they must recognise the difficult moral and practical dilemma that the issue presents.

A preparedness to compromise does not imply an absence of principle. In its proper sense, compromise only has a meaning in the context of original principle. To come to an agreement that is uninformed by principle is not compromise but expediency, and has no moral basis whatever. Only when one is clear about the principle at stake can one decide whether compromise is justified.

This consideration was foremost in the minds of myself and my colleagues in Government at the time of the Falklands invasion in 1982. Some people levelled the accusation at the Government, and at Margaret Thatcher in particular, that we were determined to resort to military means at all costs. This is not true: we were all mindful of the price in human life that would be paid even in a successful operation. We had to decide at an early point where the dividing line between principle and compromise should be drawn. It was our view, supported by the vast majority of people in Britain, that the Falkland Islands were sovereign British territory, illegally invaded by the Argentines and occupied by them without the consent of the islanders. We resolved that, while we would pursue every available avenue for peace, we would not concede the sovereignty of the islands under duress and without the consent of the islanders, and we would insist on the withdrawal of the occupying force. Those principles we held sacrosanct: on others we would compromise. I worked almost night and day for several weeks to secure a peaceful settlement, but no peace was available without surrender, and we therefore resorted to military means. This course of action was not only proper but necessary.

Firm principles are vital, and knowing when to stick to them is vital. However, blindly sticking to every principle is untenable, often self-defeating and sometimes dangerous. We are back to the question of practical and subjective choices. Individuals not only have differing principles, but differing notions of when to stand firm and when to give way. No one can lay down laws of universal behaviour in these matters. It is a question of balance, in which the moral choice must be conditioned by the likely practical consequences of alternative courses of action.

There are also situations where two principles conflict. The question of abortion presents me with this particular dilemma. On the one hand, I am opposed to abortion, except on some medical and psychological grounds. Apart from the question of when life begins, I believe there is a moral need to accept the consequences of our own actions. I feel that the most decisive way in which we demean our moral core is through wanting to have the best of every world by taking free decisions and then evading the consequences. This is true of most abortions, or of a father refusing to accept responsibility for an illegitimate birth, or of hasty divorces, or of default on a debt, or of the wish both to break the law and to avoid the penalty, or of a countless number of other situations. That is one belief.

But the second belief is that individuals must be free to form their own moral judgments. If a woman feels it is morally defensible to have an abortion, should I vote to make it illegal? I think not. If it were the case that, by supporting abortion, I was actually causing it to happen (as would be the case, for example, with capital punishment), I might think again. But in this instance I am not causing it to happen; I am merely not preventing it from happening where a woman and a doctor believe it to be justified. In these circumstances, I believe my second principle should take precedence over the first.

The same sort of conflict is involved in the more general question of the relationship between individual freedom and the protection of society. In recent decades, the prevailing view has been that individuals should be free to behave as they wish as long as this does not impinge on the freedom of others. That is a useful starting point, and one that I share, but it does not provide a definitive resolution to many issues.

Consider the questions posed by the law that compels motorists to wear seat-belts. I opposed this move when it was first suggested. I felt it was an infringement of individual liberty, because no harm to other people was involved. Yet I realised later that this view, though true in a narrow sense, was not ultimately true: vicarious damage *was* done to other people. The absence of seat-belts increased the number and the seriousness of motoring injuries, thereby stretching the resources of the Health Service and, however tenuously, diverting resources from other areas. The issue also involved a question of scale. Should one take the view that any diminution of freedom, however small, offends equally against the principle? Can one equate the compulsory wearing of seat-belts with limiting freedom of speech? I think not. Scale has to be an admissible factor. In this way, I came to accept that saving Health Service resources was a tolerable justification for a minor inconvenience like wearing a seat-belt, whereas almost any price would be too high for losing freedom of speech. I changed my mind and supported the legislation.

This issue may seem trivial, but it demonstrates the complex balance between freedom and protection. The complexity derives from the fact that the abuse of freedom is a concomitant of the existence of freedom. If one set out to eradicate all abuses, one would be forced eventually to eradicate all freedom. Everyone would like to see a society without crime, for example, but most of the means required to achieve it would be unacceptable to us. On the whole, I would rather that Governments erred on the side of caution in restricting the abuses of freedom and that we learnt to be more tolerant of the side-effects. It is an axiom that freedom is more conspicuous by its absence than its presence. The road of restriction is an easy one for Governments to tread, because it often enjoys popular support when current abuses are publicised, but it is a dangerous road. I have always supported protective legislation where minority rights are being trampled and where children are being exploited, but beyond that the ground becomes more treacherous. I prefer to keep a healthy scepticism about the notion that a Government knows what is best for people, or can successfully protect us from ourselves.

The balance between freedom and protection also involves the question of means and ends, which strikes at the heart of the moral debate on nuclear defence. Everyone has the same end in view: a peaceful world which never again experiences the use of nuclear weapons and, preferably, where such weapons do not exist. Few things annoy me more than the assumption of some peace campaigners that they are the only people who care about peace. The fact is that there are two opposed views about the best means to achieve this end. Both are sincere. Neither is indefensible. No one can say with certainty which is the more likely to be successful, but we must all reach our own conclusions.

Some people argue that, even if the continued existence of a

Western nuclear capability made war less likely, it would still be wrong because the possession of nuclear weapons is indefensible in itself. I cannot accept this view. I do not believe that the end always justifies the means, but neither do I believe that undesirable means are never justified. Once again, I reject moral absolutes and insist that a moral course of action must take practical considerations into account. The relevant questions are, first, how important is the end and what would happen if it was not achieved and, second, what are the consequences and side-effects of the proposed means to achieve it? Somewhere in the answers to these questions will lie one's personal resolution as to whether the means justify the end in any given case. On this issue, I believe that the overriding need is to avert war, and since I think that the continued possession of nuclear weapons by the West is more likely to achieve this objective than their unilateral abandonment, I contend that the means do justify the end and that my position is morally defensible.

No one has a monopoly on morality and, for that matter, no one has a monopoly on truth either. The dividing line between truth and falsity is thin at the best of times and, since many people believe that politicians have yet to discover its existence, it deserves close consideration.

If I state a fact I know to be untrue, or deny a fact I know to be true, I am lying. If I dissemble about my opinions or intentions, I am also lying, or at any rate not being entirely candid. But if I state that British industry is more efficient than it was five years ago, I am telling neither truth nor lie, but merely expressing an opinion. I may have facts and feelings to support my contention, but those who hold the opposite view will also have facts and feelings at their disposal. Most allegations of political lies stem from a misuse of language. 'The truth is' has become a substitute for 'it is my opinion' and 'a cynical lie' for 'I don't agree with you'.

The healthy process of political argument should be about the different conclusions reached by different people on a range of issues. We all start with a given series of facts, but those facts do not amount to the truth: they are neutral data from which one must form a judgment, especially as the facts often contradict each other. The basis of political debate is trying to convince other people that one's own perception and interpretation of the facts is correct. It is a battle for hearts and minds. It is usually a truthful battle in terms of individual morality, but it does not and cannot deal in objective truths. We do ourselves a great disservice both by disparaging each other's motives and by assuming that there is a 'truth' – and thus, by definition, that all else is false – when in fact all of us are making subjective attempts to form the best judgments we can.

The most grotesque farrago of 'truths', 'lies' and calumnies arises whenever there is an election. Here, every party is subject to the Catch 22 of politics. If it produces policies that reflect a minority view, it is attacked for ignoring the wishes of the people. If it produces popular policies, it is accused of bribing the electorate. If, as a Government, that party enacts its programme in detail, it is labelled as doctrinaire. If it fails to enact all of its programme, it is said to have cynically deceived the voters.

All this is grist to the mill of political debate and one should not be too sanctimonious about it. But it does conceal some important issues. I see nothing wrong in politicians trying to give people what they want – in broad terms, that is the object of the exercise – as long as it is practical, affordable, in the national interest and compatible with other priorities. If it is not, as is sometimes the case, the motive is not always cynical. Perhaps more often it is merely naive.

A reasonable analogy might be with a builder who promises to finish his work by a certain date. When he fails to meet the deadline, one wonders whether he made a knowingly false statement in order to get the job, or whether his desire to be helpful made him promise what he could not deliver. The answer is seldom apparent, but there comes a point, after two or three such occasions, when one no longer cares what it is: the sheer fact of sustained unreliability is enough to make one look for another builder. It is when one finds that all builders are much the same that confidence finally collapses. A similar process happens in politics.

In the past, some elections have had the flavour of an auction, each side trying to outbid the other in the lavishness of promises paraded. Although this practice has subsided, it remains a permanent danger. It may be due more to over-optimism than to dishonesty, but that does not make it any more acceptable. The fact still remains that, in order to be honest with other people, one must first be honest with oneself. That can be very difficult. I doubt whether anyone wholly succeeds in identifying his or her own motives, and in disentangling self-interest from objective concern.

This problem confronted me when I had to face such difficult issues as the circumstances in which a Minister ought to resign and, more recently, the extent to which I should make public my disagreement with some aspects of Government policy. Ministerial resignation is a difficult area, because it almost always involves a conflict between conscience and self-interest and thus makes one doubt one's own motives. What is more, there can be no universal resolution to the problem. If every Minister who was in some disagreement with Government policy was to resign, all Ministers would at some time or other have cause to resign – including, I might add, Prime Ministers. That would be ridiculous. But if every Minister always went along with the majority view, whatever their personal opinion of it, no Minister would ever resign over an issue of policy. That would be palpably wrong. The only conclusion one can reach is that there can be no hard and fast rules and that each Minister must draw a subjective line.

Let me say where I draw that line. Given my views on the need for a diversity of opinion and the deadening effect of unanimity, I can see no merit in every member of a Government holding identical views. If a wide range of views should exist among the MPs of any party, a similar range of views – if somewhat narrower – should exist within a Government, otherwise all Governments would be drawn from a limited sector of one party. I believe that a Cabinet Minister must be in basic agreement with the central objectives of Government policy, but this need not imply a consensus on the implementation of those objectives.

However, in addition to participation in overall policy, each Minister is directly responsible for a particular Department or area of Government business, and here I believe there is less latitude for dissent. The Minister is personally responsible for implementing policy within the Department and for explaining it to the public, and this cannot be done effectively, let alone with integrity, if the Minister disagrees with the policy.

In my case, I never seriously considered resigning from Mar-

garet Thatcher's Government over issues of general policy. As I
have already made clear, I do not like the style of the Government,
nor the tone it adopts in presenting and debating policy, and I
disagree with certain aspects of policy. But I remain a firm
supporter of the Government's objectives and of much that it has
achieved. I am no more at odds with Margaret Thatcher's policies
than she was with Ted Heath's, and I saw no more reason to
resign than she did. In both cases, we supported the Government's basic aims.

The one occasion when I might have resigned was in 1980
when, as Secretary of State for Defence, I had a major row with
the Prime Minister and the Treasury over their proposed cuts in
defence expenditure. I was convinced they were wrong on both
defence and political grounds, and I think subsequent events
proved me right. As it happens, I won the argument. Had I lost it, I
would have resigned, because the Cabinet would have overruled
me on a fundamental matter for which I was primarily responsible, and I would not have felt able to implement the decision
myself or to have defended it publicly. But on no other occasion
was there a serious gulf between my own convictions and Government policy on any of the Departments for which I was at various
time responsible.

Similar questions are raised when one considers how much a
Minister, or any MP who belongs to the governing party, should
publicly dissent from Government policy. Here, I believe that the
rules must be different for a Minister than for an MP.

For a Minister, the extremes of possible behaviour are again
equally unacceptable. It is undesirable that Ministers should have
no latitude to make public statements that differ from one another,
or that all decisions should be taken in private enclave with no hint
to the outside world of the divergent views that were submerged
in the final consensus. However, if each Minister had free licence
to expose and exploit all differences within the Government, the
necessary sense of coherence and mutual endeavour would
evaporate and the Government would become fractious and
destructive. Tony Benn provides a good example of how a
Minister can undermine his own Government in this way.

Again, there is no definitive answer, so let me explain how I
approached the problem. Contrary to the impression that some

people wish to create, I am saying nothing different now from what I was saying as a member of the Government. I was not a quiescent Minister who became a rebel when sacked: I was not a lamb then, and I am not a lion now. It is true, however, that the way in which I have expressed my views has changed since I left the Government – defensibly so, in my opinion.

In Government, my main concern was for policy and administration in the areas for which I was responsible, and it was these areas that occupied my private conversations with the Prime Minister. My views on overall Government policy were made known in three ways: to a limited audience in Cabinet discussion, in private memoranda to the Prime Minister and occasionally in public speeches. The tone of these speeches was guarded, as it had to be, but the meaning was clear and was reported accurately in the Press. I had no desire then to lead a faction in the Government and I have no desire now to lead a faction in the party: I do not like factions. The issue is one of personal independence. Just as I believe that everyone else should make their views known, I want to make my own views known, in whatever way seems best to do so and without being accused of high treason.

In Government, I thought the correct approach was to speak plainly in private and more cautiously in public. As a backbencher, I can only affect the Government through public means and see no good reason to be cryptic or elliptical. I am saying nothing substantially different from what I have always said, from what a great many Conservatives are saying, or from what most Conservatives have believed for well over a century. My circumstances may give a prominence to my views that they would not otherwise receive, but the alternatives are either to say nothing or to assert what I do not believe. In a similar position, I find it hard to imagine Margaret Thatcher keeping quiet, nor would I expect her to do so.

The position of a Minister or ex-Minister on this question is entangled with the doctrine of collective Cabinet responsibility. My interpretation of this doctrine stems from my earlier remarks on how closely a Minister should conform to Government policy and how freely dissent should be expressed in public. In my case, I feel bound, then and now, to support the Government's objectives: they are my objectives also, and I want to promote them. I also feel bound, then and now, to defend the decisions that were taken affecting Departments I was running: again, they accord with my own convictions. But I do not feel bound, then or now, to support every other aspect of Government policy in private or even in public. I do not feel responsible for policy decisions with which I disagreed at the time and with which I still disagree, especially as some of them were not taken in full Cabinet. Those of my colleagues who assert that I have no right to criticise anything the Government did while I was a member of it are asserting an absurdity. They might also recall that Margaret Thatcher built her own platform through sustained criticism of Ted Heath's Government, of which she had been a member. I do not deny her right to do so, although it might have been more helpful had she expressed her concerns in Cabinet at the time. She did not feel debarred from retrospective dissociation, which is rather more than I am claiming.

All this has to be a matter for individual judgment. Others may have different views on whether I should have resigned, whether I should have been more vociferous in Government and whether I should be less critical now. There is a tendency for people's views on the proprieties of these matters to depend on whether they agree with what I say, thus revealing the subjectivity of the question. And that really is my entire point through all these instances of moral conflicts in political life: that the resolution must be subjective rather than objective, personal rather than universal, relative rather than absolute and practical rather than theoretical. So far I have used concrete examples to show how my own experience has led me to this view. However, my religious and philosophical beliefs lead me to the same conclusion.

Morality can only have meaning in terms of the individual. I do not see how groups, whether a particular Government or society at large, can possess a corporate morality – or lack one – that is distinct from the individual morality of the people who compose it. Morality exists in the sense of difference between right and wrong, however defined, that is only to be found in individual consciousness. Since the sense resides in the individual, its interpretation will vary because each human being is necessarily different. The nature of a moral sense makes it insusceptible to collectivism. Society may need to reach a consensus on many moral issues in order to protect itself, and that consensus is and must be enforced as law on everybody, but nothing on earth can make the individual subscribe to that consensus in his or her inner self, if conscience rebels against it. For all these reasons, morality must be subjective and personal, and not objective and universal.

The reason why it is also practical and relative is slightly different. We live life in practice, in day-to-day reality, and not in theory. The concomitant of the individual's right to moral choice is the acceptance of the consequences of those choices. If we make free decisions and then reject their consequences, we have robbed them of their moral value. Therefore, I do not see how one can avoid taking practicalities into account when facing the moral issues involved in a decision. Once that happens, one cannot escape making choices that are practical and relative rather than theoretical and absolute. I have already shown that the insistence on a particular principle can have a diametrically opposite effect to that intended. Can one really argue that such an effect, or its possibility, is irrelevant to how one approaches the original principle?

The main objection to this argument is that it could be used to justify any iniquity. The individual can use the defence of personal conviction or of practical necessity to condone any action undertaken. But this raises the question of who passes judgment. We can all give our opinions – and politicians need to do so – on the words and deeds of others, but none of us can pass final judgment on them, nor even hope to know the motives that prompt them. Sometimes it is hard enough to know them in ourselves. Purity of heart is the ultimate test, and that is for God and not man to judge. One of the most arrogant features of the age is our presumption to pass moral judgment on our fellow human beings, and to believe that judgment to be final.

What, then, of those who are the intermediaries between God and man? Religion and politics are both as old as mankind itself, and the relationship between them has been a bone of contention for just as long. Throughout Western Europe, the tide of secularism has rolled inexorably forward over the centuries. Once religion occupied the central role in individual lives and in national life. It has now been relegated so far towards the fringe that people question whether Churchmen have the right to express opinions on political issues, let alone be directly involved in them. Religion has come to occupy a position of marginal importance in life.

In reality, this situation is absurd. Religion cannot be of marginal importance: it is either of absolute importance or of no importance at all. Its current position is a false compromise between faith and the lack of it, more especially the latter as personal religious instincts have become buried deeper and deeper under the dross of our rational, empirical age.

Of course Churchmen should be free to express public views about all aspects of life, including politics. How can they do otherwise, especially as politics have invaded so much of life? Without entering a pointless debate as to whether Christ was a 'politician' or a 'revolutionary', it seems to me that the fundamental point is that Christ loved and loves individual people for what we are and understands, in anything but an abstract way, the practical problems and hard choices we all encounter in the world, while guiding us to His way of life. I believe that this same quality has inspired all the truly great Church leaders throughout history: a deep love for the whole of humanity and a true concern for mankind as it is, and not just as it might be or ought to be. It is through this transcendent love that such people have achieved that remarkable combination of utter moral conviction and true humility that the rest of us find so impossible to attain.

So I do not see how the Church can stand aside from politics. I do not see how individual Churchmen can ignore such profound moral issues as nuclear weapons. Clergymen do not exist to make life comfortable for us, and I do not think they can avoid a responsibility to interpret Christ's teaching in our daily lives. Nor do I think that this point is invalidated by the fact that, within the Churches, there will be different views on all these issues. Indeed, such divergence is confirmation of the fact that morality is not absolute and that it stems from individual conscience. Thus, within each Church, there are differences on the nuclear issue. Thus the various Churches in Britain and Argentina took different views on the Falklands War. Thus we all need guidance and help to come to conclusions which we can defend, while never forgetting our susceptibility to error.

It comes down to individual moral standards. More important than where one's conscience leads is the fact that conscience itself is important. Honest intention and personal integrity are what matter most: they are the compass and lodestone of life, without which one is truly adrift. For politicians, the need to hold fast to them is especially great because the perils and temptations are considerable, the lines always blurred at the edges.

Many people, myself included, believe that moral and spiritual values have declined as material values have increased. I am not an ascetic, but I believe that society does not have the balance right at present. I suspect that there will be – perhaps already is – a revival in spiritual values, and that people will return, with some relief, to a more disciplined life and less material attitude. I hope that it will not take the form of a bogus certainty and an intolerant rectitude.

There is always the risk in discussing morality at all that one will appear priggish and insufferably virtuous. I hope I have not done so: I certainly do not feel that I am. Of course, in our hearts, we all need to believe that our own moral values are the right ones – how could we live otherwise? But it is still possible to acknowledge the different standards of others, even if one dissents from them, and it is always dangerous to assume one's own superiority and to invite the hubris that usually accompanies it. No one has a monopoly on morality. All that is important is that we should find our own values and try to be faithful to them.

SEVEN

What Kind of Society?

'In civilised society, we all depend upon each other.' – SAMUEL
JOHNSON

wet, adj. containing, soaked with, covered with, water or other
liquid: tearful: grown in damp soil: given to drinking, or tipsy
(slang): ineffectual, or crazy (slang).

dry, adj. deficient in moisture, sap, rain: enforcing or subjected
to prohibition: uninteresting: frigid, precise, formal: of manner, distantly unsympathetic.

(extracts from *Chambers 20th Century Dictionary*)

Whenever the wets raise the subject of unemployment, we are
taken to task by certain newspapers and by some of our colleagues. The criticism comes in two parts. We are reminded that,
in the battle to revive British industry and restore national
prosperity, inflation is a greater evil than unemployment and must
be conquered first. We are also lectured on the infirmity of
courting easy public sympathy by expressing concern for the
unemployed, when we have no alternative economic policy to
offer.

These criticisms ignore the fact that the dispute between wet
and dry does not only concern economic policy, but – just as
important – the balance between economic policy and social
policy. To insist that unemployment is an urgent social problem
in need of immediate and imaginative attention may or may not
require a new economic policy, but it undoubtedly requires a
sympathetic social policy. Even in these materialistic times,
Governments are not merely Directorates of Economic Policy.
Most economic theories have damaging social consequences if
pushed to their extremes, which is why economic purism is
dangerous to Governments. Most people do not want Britain to

be the richest and most efficient country in the world, if the penalty is widespread hopelessness and a divided nation. They would rather strike a balance between economic and social needs. For that reason, I am inclined to think that 'wet' stands for What Everybody Thinks.

The balance between economic and social policy is always hard to maintain when economic growth is lacking and pressure is put upon Government expenditure. In these circumstances, there is a temptation to argue that economic recovery is so important that it should take precedence over everything else. Indeed, some would argue that if one can encourage a thriving and competitive economy, which encourages and rewards individual effort, social policy will take care of itself and require only marginal Government involvement.

I do not share this outlook. I think it undesirable for any Government to make a hard and fast choice, or to appear to do so, between economic and social policy. If the present Government errs in over-emphasising economic policy, a Labour Government would err in over-emphasising social policy, with equally harmful effects.

Governments cannot neglect social policy for one reason. Come what may in the world around us, there is a permanent need for Britain to remain a harmonious nation, united within herself. We will not always be rich, or successful, or powerful, or at peace, however much we want to be and try to be; but we will, for all time, be living together on the same islands, dealing with each other and needing to get on with each other. That will only be possible – only ever has been possible, here or anywhere else – if there is a broad agreement within the nation on the nature of our society and a belief that it conforms to the prevailing concepts of fairness and justice.

This leads to a second and more contemporary reason not to neglect social policy. However much one accepts – and I do accept – the need for wealth to be created, the need for individual enterprise to be rewarded and the need for everyone to have a free choice in how they spend their money, there remains another need: to use economic wealth, not only as an end in its own right, but as a means to the improvement of society as a whole. There will always be ways to improve social conditions, and most people will always believe that some of the increase in national wealth should be used for that purpose. This reflects a wise instinct that, if we allow individual acquisitiveness to be the rampant motive, we will eventually destroy society. The very word society implies sharing values, not purely individual ones.

For these reasons, social policy should never be subservient to economic policy. However, the second reason dictates that the reverse should not be the case either. Increased wealth is a pre-condition of social improvement, and therefore has to be created. One of our problems is that we have become so conditioned to expect social improvement that we have forgotten its dependence on created wealth.

A period of relative economic failure produces social pressures. That is unavoidable. It equally tends to produce two conflicting orthodoxies, one arguing that most of the effort should be directed towards the cause (the economic argument), the other that it should be directed towards the effect (the social argument). In dissenting from both orthodoxies, I do not reject the intrinsic validity of either, but the implication that a choice has to be made between them. Economic and social needs should be complementary, not competitive: they must be pursued in parallel, whether times are good, bad or indifferent.

With this in mind, I would like to consider society today, where it is going, what the problems are and how they might be overcome. These questions are conditioned by the view one takes of society itself. There are three main political views available: the Marxist view, the laissez-faire view and the paternalist view. I am aware that paternalism is now the least fashionable of the three, but since I hope it will become fashionable again, I would rather call it by its proper name than hide behind a euphemism. In vindicating the paternalist view, I want to explain why the other two are misguided and inadequate.

The Marxist fallacy starts by regarding society as an abstract and impersonal unit, rather than as a collection of individuals. That is why doctrinaire Socialists find social engineering such a comfortable concept. The very phrase implies that society can be approached as a raw lump of metal, capable of being beaten and bent into a finished artefact. It also implies a definite idea as to what final shape that artefact should take.

This is literally an inhuman view. I can think of no adequate way to describe society other than as the sum total of individuals, ideas and feelings that exist in any one community at any one moment. This definition expresses three beliefs: that society is founded on the individual, that it varies from one place to another and that it varies from one time to another. Upon the recognition of individuality is built the acceptance that each person has a different contribution to make to society, and that each contribution should be appreciated. Upon the recognition of place is built the acceptance that different communities will form different views of society: no single concept can be shared throughout the world. Upon the recognition of time is built the acceptance that people change – not in basic nature, perhaps, but in the ideas and feelings which they express.

Because I view society in this way, I cannot believe in a notion like 'the ideal society'. Such a concept can exist only in the imagination. If society contains a wide diversity of individuals, each with a mixture of human strengths and weaknesses, it may be comparatively good or bad in any particular place or time, but how can it possibly be ideal? Moreover, if society is constantly changing, what would happen if it should attain this 'ideal'? Belief in an ideal society must be based on belief in a static society, transformed by ideology from static impurity to static purity. I do not believe that such an outlook bears any approximation to reality.

No one could accuse the laissez-faire view of falling into these traps. But, in its proclamation of individual values and virtues, it perpetrates its own fallacy: that life is fair and therefore that, if left to its own devices, it will create a fair society. The heyday of laissez-faire philosophy was Victorian England and it is not surprising that, in an age when economic laissez-faire has become fashionable once more, the cry should be heard for a return to Victorian moral values. Even allowing for the fact that we are presumably being urged to accept the more positive aspects of Victorian morality (hard work, thrift, importance of the family, cleanliness) rather than its more debatable features (hypocritical rectitude, rigidity, repression and widespread – though not universal – indifference to social suffering), I find it impossible to share its tenets and the social attitudes that it encourages.

It is dangerous to pick and choose between different aspects of the same entity, since they tend to be bound up with each other. I am not convinced it is possible to have the strengths of Victorian morality, while dispensing with its less attractive side. Victorian morality was based on the type of absolute, universal, objective and theoretical values that I criticised in the previous chapter. That is why it caused such hideous practical difficulties and why I am suspicious of it. I feel that it positively discourages one from seeing, let alone tolerating, other perspectives on life.

Any successful person who was brought up to believe that the rewards of life will come to those who are good and dutiful and conscientious and able, must feel that life is indeed a vindication of that belief. And so it is. For that person. But for thousands of other people, equally good, dutiful, conscientious and able, life does not work out like that. In its distribution of material rewards, triumphs and disasters, life is unfair and arbitrary. Indeed, if the laissez-faire view was correct and life was truly fair and individual virtue perfectly rewarded, the whole moral value of life would be subverted. Virtue would bring its own reward instead of being its own reward. Self-sacrifice would become meaningless.

If one believes that life is broadly fair, one will believe that politics should encourage this natural justice. If one believes, as I do, that it is arbitrary and often unfair, one will believe that politics should help to compensate for this. The distinction was made differently in a recent article by Paul Johnson, who welcomed the demise of people like myself, whose political attitudes he assumed to be conditioned by some 'silver-spoon' guilt, and our replacement by people who had grown up in a harder school, who had forced their way to the top on ability alone, and whose attitudes were less likely to be tinged by these alleged negative feelings. This is an interesting point of view.

To begin with, I do not accept that someone who has had to struggle to the top necessarily has a 'stand on your own two feet' mentality, nor do I accept that someone who has been born into relatively affluent circumstances necessarily feels guilty about it. Many distinguished national figures over the years have risen from poor backgrounds, but have retained a full awareness of how life might have been for them and how it still is for other people. At the other end of the spectrum, there is a distinction to be made between guilt and the awareness of good fortune. I do not feel at all guilty about my circumstances, any more than I feel envious of those who have more than I do, but I am aware of having been more fortunate than most. This is not a negative or unhealthy attitude, and I think that the habit of sneering at political paternalism is most unattractive.

'Awareness of good fortune' is the operative phrase, and it applies equally to the chance of one's background, to the chance of the individual gifts one is given, and to the chance of the success one attains. I may have had a head-start over most people by the background I was arbitrarily given; other people have equally had a head-start by the talents they were arbitrarily given; others still have had a head-start through sheer good luck. This gives us all cause to be thankful, but not to be either guilty or arrogant. We do not create our own talents, any more than we create our own backgrounds, and the strength of character that makes us build on what we are given instead of letting it go to waste is not necessarily of our own making either. Nor are the rewards that may or may not attend our efforts.

These observations have a decisive effect on one's attitude to political issues, and especially to unemployment. If one believes that life rewards virtue and ability, it is difficult not to feel that the companies that go broke and the people who lose their jobs somehow deserve to do so, while successful people and successful companies deserve their success. My conclusions are different. Many bad companies have undoubtedly crashed in the recession, and many incompetent or irresponsible people have lost their jobs. Equally, there are bad companies still in business and good companies out of business, and whether good or bad employees lose or keep their jobs in consequence is principally a matter of luck. Admittedly, the most able and energetic people are always more likely to find employment than those who are less gifted, but this raises a separate question. The most able and energetic people are not necessarily, for example, the best parents, the most considerate members of the community or those who bring most pleasure to other people – all of which are as important to the well-being of the nation as a whole as specific job skills. I do not suggest that material reward should be related to these less tangible virtues, but an awareness of the fact that different people have different contributions to make to society helps one to see economic issues in a broader context.

All this leads me to the view that, whereas I do not believe that people unfortunate enough to be out of work should be offered false hopes, neither do I think they should be regarded as the victims of their own inadequacies and left to get on with life as best they can. No one is an island: we all need help in one way or another.

I therefore reject both the Marxist and laissez-faire views of society. Both are insensitive to place and time. Marxism takes no account of the British belief in individual freedom and independence, while laissez-faire ignores both our sense of social responsibility and our preference for sensible compromise. I wish neither to impose a false uniformity on individuals in the search for an imaginary ideal, nor to allow individualism to ride roughshod over wider social needs in the mistaken belief that life is fair. Instead, I believe that society needs to maintain a balance between the legitimate self-expression of its individual members and the harmony of the whole, and that Governments should intervene, in a practical and sensible way, to restrain unbridled self-interest and to improve social conditions in the nation. That is the meaning of paternalism and I see no reason to be ashamed of it. Indeed, it has been the predominant view in the Conservative Party for most of the last century.

Paternalists favour an approach that is both realistic and caring. Instead of starting with an ideal and trying to draw reality up to meet it, we start with reality and seek ways of improving it. We need permanently to be aware of the shortcomings in society, as they change over time, and attempt to remedy them. Since there is no ideal, we can never arrive at an end point, but we can always travel hopefully. The answer to the question 'what kind of society do we want to build?' is therefore vague – 'a better one'.

In defining 'better' at any moment, there are three abiding needs that a Government should take into account: the need for national unity, the need for individual responsibility and the need for social improvement. I want to examine each of these in the light of current social problems.

The need for national unity comes first. The scope for division and conflict within a nation is as great as it is between nations. All societies include the seeds of their own destruction: latent elements that, if they are not contained, could tear them apart. Such explosions have happened in many countries through history – including Britain, albeit mildly – and the consequences are always grievous, both for individuals and for the nation. The preservation of national unity and social cohesion is thus a major obligation on any Government. This unity must be based on responsible individuality and not on uniformity. People know they are unique as individuals and are proud to be so. They know that they possess some aptitudes and attributes and lack others. What they cannot do individually, and what Governments must help to do, is to harness this diversity effectively, so that everyone feels a valued part of the whole.

National unity is a relative concept, not an absolute one. Different circumstances release different forces, tending towards or away from unity. A war or shared sense of national crisis, whatever the evils involved, tends to promote unity. A widespread sense of individual rejection or inability to contribute tends to undermine unity. That is why unemployment is such a real threat to the nation.

To illustrate the divisive nature of mass unemployment, one must first look at its human source: an individual redundancy. When a factory closes down and someone loses a job, at first there is a natural sense of shock. This tends to be followed by a brief feeling of release and euphoria. This is followed by a period of wondering what to do next, and whether another job will come along. When it does not, depression sets in. The person feels both unwanted and bored. There is a sense of bitterness and despair. There seems to be no hope.

On an individual level, this hopelessness is tragic, and I do not see why politicians should be ashamed to say so, whether they can cure it immediately or not. It is a curious set of values that regards all expressions of feeling as weakness. However, the problem does not remain on an individual level. It affects different communities and it does not affect them equally. There are still many regions where the percentage of people unemployed is in single figures, but there are others, especially at the heart of major cities, where it is as high as thirty, forty or even fifty per cent. Within these communities, it may run higher still in certain sectors of the population – especially among young people and racial minorities. That is what makes national statistics such an unreliable indicator of social realities.

The problem is more than the sum total of individual despair, because the scale of the issue creates added pressures. Amongst its by-products are a gradual withholding of consent from the Government, signs of a rejection of civilised values, an increase in crime and lawlessness and occasional outbreaks of anger and frustration, as evidenced in the riots of 1981. I do not in any way condone such lawlessness, but I can understand it. The foundation of law is justice, and the law will only be obeyed if there is acceptance of the justice on which it is based. If this consensus collapses, so will the law. That is why national unity is not just a noble ideal, but a practical necessity. The preservation of unity requires much skill and sympathy on the part of politicians, especially at times like these, and it must be the first social priority of any Government.

I feel that the mistake made by this Government is to believe that, because they cannot wave a magic wand to solve the problem, there is nothing they can do or say to make it better. As a result, there are at least three million people who are not only unable to find work through no fault of their own, but who can see no prospect of finding work and who are inclined to feel that they are neglected and forgotten, while others grow wealthier around them. 'On yer bike' is not the most constructive advice in these circumstances. It may be a reasonable thing to say to any individual, but not to three million of them. That is why the individual values of self-help cannot literally be translated into the national values of a Government. For the same reason, I am concerned by the priority given to tax cuts at a time of such pressure on the social services. I am not persuaded by the argument that relatively small cuts in personal taxation do much to encourage business initiative. A doubtful economic gain must be outweighed by a definite social loss.

I accept that any action to reduce unemployment will be gradual in effect but, in the meantime, the Government must show its concern on the issue and the importance it attaches to remedying it. A sense of hopelessness in the nation is the ultimate failure of statesmanship. The way to alleviate it in the short term is to mitigate its worst effects, to be generous with those who are affected, and to demonstrate that the underlying issues are being tackled decisively and imaginatively. At the moment, only the first of these is happening.

Unemployment may be the most immediate threat to national unity, but it is not the only one. Race relations are another, and one that I particularly want to mention because they illustrate that national unity is not compatible with rigid insistence on any principles, no matter how noble they may be. It is now accepted by most people that a tight control on immigration is the only way to make harmonious race relations possible in Britain. Yet, for much of the 1960s and early 1970s, the whole of the liberal establishment and a great many politicians believed precisely the opposite, despite clear public opinion to the contrary. Their motives were praiseworthy, yet their views were unacceptable, because they did not listen to other people, they were unprepared to admit to the pressure caused by high immigration on local communities and they tried to force their own views on to everyone else.

As a result of the failure to curb immigration at an earlier stage, the pressures on race relations – which are what really matter – were greater than they need have been. Only now, after several years of control, are some of those pressures being alleviated, but they are still considerable and are aggravated by the recession. We cannot allow racial minorities to become alienated from national life, any more than we can allow it for other minorities. At the same time, preferential treatment for any minority will justifiably anger others who suffer and who are not so preferred. Once again, we must seek a balance. We should help everyone who is disadvantaged, but in a way that is even-handed and is seen to be fair. It will take a long time to achieve a true multi-racial society, and there will be many difficulties to come. As always, it is imperative to listen to people, whether one likes what they say or not. Racial prejudice will not be overcome by pretending that it does not exist. We must ensure that national unity is not further strained on this issue.

After national unity, the next need is for individual responsibility. If we wish to live in a free society, we each have to accept a personal responsibility for upholding its values and its freedoms. We should rely on government to do things that we are unable to do for ourselves, but if we rely on government to do everything we are both abdicating our responsibility and forfeiting our freedom. I feel that we have started to take too much for granted, and to be too lazy in defence of our values. Because we have grown used to our freedoms, we assume that they will always exist and that, if we cannot be bothered to uphold them, somebody else will. It is much the same attitude that, in the area of defence, favours British disarmament and a reliance on others to defend us. It is difficult to exaggerate the dangers of such an attitude.

One example of this abdication of responsibility is our reaction to the rising crime rate. There is a constant clamour for the Government to 'do something' about it. How often do we pause to think whether there is anything *we* can do about it? We need to consider why there has been such a steep increase in crime. I have suggested that the boredom and despair caused by unemployment is one factor, but I do not regard it as the major factor in a trend that has continued for several decades, irrespective of economic conditions. I believe the major factor to be a decline in discipline within society. Since the war, parents have brought their children up less strictly. The ethos of the times, promulgated by the media and supported by education, has been in favour of a more liberal society with less discipline. I do not blame the media or the schools for this; they may have encouraged the process, but they were reflecting a widespread feeling in society at large. Many factors were pulling in the same direction.

Over time, moral values have weakened; the influence of the Churches has weakened; the family unit has weakened. Children have much more licence – which is not the same as freedom – and at an ever earlier age. Indeed, the view has emerged that it is almost a sin to teach one's values to one's children: better that they should discover their own, since they are bound to be different anyway. This amounts to an abdication of parental responsibility, of which the consequences are a lack of self-discipline, personal insecurity and, in the end, lawlessness. On top of this have come the pressures of mass unemployment.

I am not attacking the move to a more relaxed and free society, in fact I welcome it. I am attacking the breakdown in individual discipline and responsibility that have accompanied it. We have treated freedom as an absolute, rather than as a balance between the opposite extremes of repression and anarchy. Freedom can only exist within a framework of order and regulation. In the outer world of society, the enemies of freedom are an excess of order and an absence of order; in the inner world of the individual, they are a repressed personality and an undisciplined character. Without discipline, freedom cannot be attained, either for society or for the individual. It is our failure to recognise this truth that has led us astray and has made us misuse the new liberties we enjoy instead of benefiting from them.

That is why there have been calls for the return to a more rigid society, based on Victorian values. This merely confirms the habitual tendency of society to swing from one extreme to the other. The Victorian era reflected the evils of the opposite extreme: an excess of order in the outer world and an excess of repression in the inner world. Possibly one reason that the pendulum has swung too far now is that it swung too far the other way then. If we allow it to swing back again, we will be no closer to a balance. The need is not to diminish freedom, but to develop self-discipline.

Paradoxically, the main cause of increasing crime lies in the homes of law-abiding citizens. In that case, the remedy lies there also. It is both right and necessary to bring children up firmly and in obedience to the ultimate values. Apart from anything else, it makes life a lot easier for the children themselves. This is not brainwashing; it is moral education. Children will still grow up to challenge their parents' values, but at least they will know what those values are. A social change of this nature will not prevent crime – nor will anything else – but it will help us to attack its major cause, instead of being forced to attack the symptoms. I welcome the increase in police strength and I support the move towards stiffer sentences for violent crime, because I believe they will have some deterrent effect. But we should not pretend that they provide a long term answer to the problem. Longer sentences should not obscure the fact that those who commit crimes have been allowed to get into the mental condition that prompts them to do so. The blame does not rest primarily with 'society', but with all of us as individuals.

There are also more immediate steps that can be taken to deter crime. We can combine with our neighbours to give more protection to our local community: much attention is now focussed on the success of neighbourhood action groups in reducing local crime. We can pay greater regard both to making our own houses more secure and to watching for open invitations to crime elsewhere. We can play our part in community groups that provide facilities for young people and help keep them out of trouble. We can encourage groups that help young offenders. We can offer assistance to victims of crime in our own neighbourhood. If we see the law being broken, we can take the trouble to act as witnesses, instead of pretending that we did not notice.

These are some of the practical steps we can take. There are many others. There is only one objection to all these measures: that they involve too much time and trouble. To that objection, there is only one answer. It does take time to support the law. It does take time to bring up a family properly. It does take time to establish a peaceful and happy community. It takes a lot of care and love as well. If we do not take the time to do these things, the crime rate will go on rising, however strong the police and however long the sentences. An orderly society does not run itself and it cannot be taken for granted. Nor can the Government guarantee it, unless every member of society plays a part. We must learn once more to uphold our values and to pass them on to our children through the family, through the community, through education and, I hope, through the Churches. Our collective future is the individual responsibility of each and every one of us.

After national unity and individual responsibility, the third need is for social improvement. There is a tendency to view this subject as a narrow process of redistributing income from the wealthy to the poor. However, in its proper sense, social improvement should concern a bettering of the quality of life for all members of society. In this context, there are three separate aspects to it. The first involves direct financial redistribution (pensions, supplementary benefits, rent rebates, etc.). The second involves the availability of services and amenities (health, education, the arts, housing, the environment, etc.). The third involves the anticipation of future changes and planning for them.

Each aspect is a major subject in its own right. The problem with all of them is a shortage of financial resources, and it is this problem that I want to consider. There are two points to make at the outset. The first is that we all want, and expect, a continuous improvement in social conditions. The second is that such improvement requires a continuous increase in resources. The squaring of this circle has been the major challenge to Governments for many years.

There are three ways in which Government resources can be increased: by a general growth in national wealth, by a rise in taxation or by borrowing. The social advances of the post-war years were financed by all three means. By the mid 1970s, none of them was available. The economic boom fizzled out some time ago and has not yet returned. The redistribution of income through taxation went as far as it sensibly could – if not too far. Further taxation of the wealthy, however attractive to Socialists, would have yielded a small incremental revenue. Increasingly, taxation was taking from the slightly above-average earner and giving to the slightly below-average earner. With the first two options closed, Governments borrowed money to the point where that option was exhausted too. In this way, the post-war social democratic consensus ran into a brick wall, which accounts for much of the subsequent debate within all political parties. It also accounts for the difficulties that have faced this Government, and which were not of its own making.

In these circumstances, I endorse both the Government's commitment to reviving national prosperity and its argument for a radical review of social funding. However, I fear that 'monetarist' policies have hindered the first and that public reaction will embitter the second, if it does not prevent it altogether. In the next chapter, I tackle the question of economic and industrial revival. Here, I would like to pursue the case for a radical review of social funding.

Whatever the rate of economic growth in the next decade or so, it is unlikely to generate sufficient resources to satisfy the growing demands of public expenditure, especially if the Government has to support a permanently high level of unemployment. Rather than accept a reduced level of public services, I would prefer to reform both the provision and the use of resources. We should examine both whence the money comes and where it goes.

The principal means of implementing social policy are through the apparatus of the Welfare State, which was developed by all political parties during the Second World War and was enacted by the 1945 Labour Government. Many things have changed since 1945, and I see no reason why the Welfare State should not be subjected to the same critical eye as everything else. It may be regarded as a sacred cow, but it is not immune to the laws of nature: the quantity of the milk depends on the quantity of the grass. When the grass runs low, we have to find other ways to keep up the milk yield.

As I see it, the Welfare State suffers from three questionable assumptions. The first is that it is the Government's duty not only to ensure the existence of good social services, but actually to provide those services itself. The second is that the benefits should be provided equally to everyone. The third is that Government spending and investment should be kept separate from private spending and investment. If these three assumptions are maintained, I believe it to be inevitable that the quality of many social services will decline, no matter which party is in power. What we have done, in attempting to resolve the political battle between capitalism and collectivism over the years, is to set up two separate systems. This is inaccurately called a mixed economy, but it is really a form of economic apartheid. I believe in the need for a mixed economy, but not in the parallel development of two systems that are prevented from mixing.

The tendency of the moderate left to view these assumptions as sacrosanct is damaging both to social policy and to their own objectives. However, a dogmatic assertion of contrary principles is not the answer, at least not my answer. Social policy should not be dominated by ideology in any form. Instead, we should be concerned with providing the best social services that we can sensibly afford in the most efficient way. That is why we should examine the feasibility of privatising some or all of the social services, with the Government providing people with money to buy their own services, rather than providing the services itself.

Despite the howls of protest that always greet this suggestion, I must insist that such a change does not intrinsically imply a reduction in social services, nor need it imply rigorous means testing. As I have made clear, I do not wish the standard of services to be reduced. Nor do I want to make their quality entirely dependent on the ability to pay. Nor do I want to live in a full-blown means test society. However, I would like to see more cost-effective services and, since privatisation is a possible way of achieving them, it ought to be examined and, if possible, implemented in one area of the country as an experiment. Even without such a radical change, I want to see Government and private industry work in partnership with each other and not in isolation and I believe that, without such a partnership, we will not be able to protect the present level of social services, let alone respond to the challenges of the future.

To summarise, I have argued the need for social policy to be diverted towards the three objectives of national unity, individual responsibility and social improvement. In highlighting the problems that affect all three objectives, I have given only an indication of what I believe the Government should do to address them. In the final section of this chapter, I want to consider its role in more detail.

I do not over-estimate the power of Government to solve deep-rooted social problems. Politicians did not cause them and they cannot cure them. However, a Government can do more than any other group of people to draw attention to the problems, to intervene to ameliorate them and to give leadership to the nation as they are gradually settled. The key word is leadership. That is the quality a Government most needs to demonstrate, particularly in times of stress. That leadership must come in three parts: in action for the present, in planning for the future, and in the attitude adopted in presenting the issues to the nation.

This raises the spectre of intervention versus laissez-faire, which so bedevils Conservative discussion on the role of government. Once again, I reject being presented with two extreme approaches and being required to make an absolute choice between them. I oppose intervention if it is based on the assumption that Whitehall knows best and if its effect is to impede what people can do for themselves. I oppose laissez-faire if it is based on the assumption that it is a virtue for a Government to do as little as possible and if its effect is to perpetuate unfairness and hardship. Instead, I prefer to think of the Government's role in terms of a partnership – working with both individuals and institutions in a practical and sensible way, in order to achieve national objectives. A Government has a public duty; it has a certain power at its disposal; it has the possibility of taking initiatives. If it is able to take an initiative or to use its power to discharge its duty, then it ought to do so – preferably in partnership with others and not by dictat. With this in mind, there are four steps that the Government should take with some urgency.

First, it should ease the overwhelming priority given to economic policy and acknowledge the importance of social policy. This request does not detract from the need to create wealth: what I seek is a balance between economic and social needs, not a different imbalance. Ministers may be upset by this remark and feel that it ignores their efforts. If so, they are partly to blame themselves, because they have been so concerned to hide their failure, as they see it, to cut public spending, that they have refused to take the credit for maintaining it. Whether fair or not, the public perception is of a Government that is indifferent to social problems and wants to cut public spending, not just out of economic necessity, but for doctrinal preference. It is this feeling that the Labour Party is exploiting and it is damaging the Government more than anything else.

Second, as part of this change of attitude, the Government should show that it attaches equal importance to national unity, social improvement and individual responsibility, instead of stressing the last of these at the expense of the other two. The approach needs to become more conciliatory.

Third, this new approach must be reflected in action and not just in words. More generous benefits should be available to the poor and to the unemployed. I am aware that the 'black economy' is thriving, that redundancy payments are often high and that the benefits received by some people out of work exceed the wages received by some people in work. But these facts tend to be portrayed as the universal reality, which they are not. If we constantly harp on the abuses of the system, we will forget those whom the system abuses. At present, the real incomes of the 'haves' and the employed are rising steadily; the real incomes of the 'have-nots' and the unemployed are at best static in absolute terms and are declining in relative terms. The Government may argue that it is madness to raise the living standards of people who are not working, and they may be right intellectually. But people do not feel with their intellects and, at present, they feel unfairly treated and with some justification. This Government may have an impressive combined IQ, but it has yet to show that its collective heart and its collective soul matches the calibre of its collective mind.

Fourth, the human aspect of unemployment must also be tackled. We must alleviate the sense of hopelessness and of inability to contribute. At present, our resources are mismatched. On the one hand, we are paying three million people to do nothing. On the other, there is great need for help in a range of social projects, from relieving urban dereliction, to providing community activities, to giving help and care to the old and disabled. When there is apparently no economic work for many people to do, why should they not perform social work? Apart from the benefit of such work to society as a whole, it would bring pride and purpose back into the lives of those who perform it. There is no reason why the Government should not work with local authorities, with voluntary associations and with private industry in helping to ensure a social return from social security.

All these measures would help to create public confidence in social policy. Upon the basis of this confidence, the Government should present the options fully and truthfully to the nation. This Government has done more than most to publicise its long term financial forecasts, but it has shied away from discussing their implications because of the fear of public reaction. This same fear has caused Ministers to be more optimistic than is justified about the prospects for recovery and for future employment, and thus to run the risk of raising public expectations above the probable reality. Few things are more damaging to the nation and more dispiriting for individuals than for hopes to be raised and then dashed.

People know there are great problems and they prefer to know what they are. They will accept that solutions are not readily available to all of them, if there is evidence of a patient desire to find them and an ability to do so eventually. They will endure hardship if it is seen to be necessary. They will accept major change if they are given time to get used to it. They believe that a discussion of the difficulties makes solutions easier to find and to accept. In other words, their feelings towards political problems are much the same as towards their own problems in life. In both cases, two temptations must be avoided: to deny a problem that exists, and to imply a solution that does not.

If enough confidence can be generated to allow the alternatives to be aired, the implementation of radical measures to reform social spending will become possible. This still remains the Government's proper objective; at present it lacks a strategy to attain it. The preceding steps are the correct strategy. If they are taken, I am confident we can improve our existing social services and respond to future demands, without extravagant government expenditure and without diminishing social values.

This will require formidable political leadership. I would like to see it directed towards the achievement of a true balance in society between the individual and the nation, a true mix between the public and private sectors and a true partnership between the Government and the governed. We all recognise the injustice of excessive state control. We must acknowledge that expecting the individual to do almost everything unaided is equally unjust and is damaging to the nation. Governments exist to ensure that the strong do not tyrannise the weak.

Over the next decade and more, we will have many challenges to face. We have enjoyed a long period of material progress and prosperity. We are now confronting the problems caused both by the end of that period of progress and by the vacuum of moral responsibility that its existence encouraged. These are not problems that economic policy alone can cure and, if economic measures are applied in a social void, they will lead to catastrophe of one sort or another. National unity and social cohesion are inevitably under pressure at the moment and that pressure will increase. It may not be possible – will not be possible – for a Government to please everyone, but if there is a genuine intention to govern on behalf of the whole nation, that intention will not go unnoticed and will help to heal incipient wounds. An open mind and a generous spirit will far outweigh the value of any dogma.

There is no reason why the bridges should not be crossed. Over the centuries, we have surmounted all manner of circumstantial obstacles. If our current problems are handled with sensitivity and imagination, we shall put them behind us as well. The manner in which we now grasp the challenge of solving them will determine, for good or ill, what kind of society we can expect in the coming decades.

Apart from politics, my great love and pastime is gardening, so I would like to conclude this chapter on a horticultural note. The proper answer to the question 'wet or dry?' lies in the soil. Dryness will produce a cactus society, scratching its members to pieces. Wetness will produce a paddy-field society, incapable of material progress. The fact that I now carry a watering can is due to the present aridity of the earth. I carry it, not to create a swamp, but to achieve a balanced soil, well watered and well nourished, that can produce an infinite variety of healthy plants, both individually unique and mutually dependent, as nature intended them to be.

EIGHT

Where 'Monetarism' Fails

'There is no permanent, absolute, unchangeable truth; what we should pursue is the most convenient arrangement of our ideas.' – SAMUEL BUTLER

10 May 1979 now seems to belong to the distant past. If a week in politics is a long time, five years is an eternity. That was the day when the Conservatives won the General Election, and 'monetarism' was installed as Government economic policy.

It is easy to see why monetary theory was attractive to politicians of all parties in the 1970s. Put simply, its proposition was that an excessive growth in the money supply (principally the amount of money printed by the Government) was the underlying cause of inflation and that, if the money supply was kept in harness with output, inflation would be contained. Since inflation was the major problem facing the British economy at the time, such a proposition was of great interest.

I have some harsh things to say about 'monetarism' in this chapter. Since my remarks will be misinterpreted by some, let me make three things clear at the outset. In my criticism of 'monetarism', I do not forget the dire economic circumstances of 1979. Nor do I dispute the link between high inflation and unemployment. Nor do I deny that control of the money supply is an important factor in economic management.

Because I remember 1979, I accept both that economic and industrial regeneration was essential and that it would have been hard to achieve under any policies, especially once the world recession had started. At that time, inflation was rampant and was increasing monthly. Excessive wage increases debilitated the competitiveness of British industry. The 'winter of discontent' suggested an underlying industrial anarchy, which the Labour Government did little to stop. There was a sense of deep-rooted malaise, which heightened the attraction of the apparent panacea of 'monetarism'. Whatever one's view of the panacea, some remedy was urgently required. I therefore do not dispute the Government's economic objectives, but merely its means of trying to achieve them.

Because I accept the link between high inflation and unemployment, I support the priority given to reducing inflation when the Government took office in 1979. A major reflation would have been disastrous, which is why the policies put forward by the Labour Party at the 1983 Election were mistaken. They would have reduced unemployment to some extent in the short term, but at the cost of higher inflation, lower productivity and even worse competitiveness. They would thus have increased unemployment in the long term. However, these remarks do not mean that rigid deflation was the answer.

Because I accept that control of the money supply is necessary, I acknowledge that some of the problems of the 1970s were caused by neglect of this factor. Wage inflation and a rise in raw material costs are not the only causes of price inflation – although, in my opinion, they remain the major causes – and greater monetary control was necessary.

Had this factor been returned to its proper place in the overall balance of the economy, no one could sensibly have objected. The fault was to place such disproportionate emphasis on the money supply that a worse imbalance was created. This resulted from an even greater fault – which is the real charge against 'monetarists' – that they took one limited factor and raised it into an ideology, oblivious of the need for balance in the economy and in disregard of changing circumstances.

Before developing this accusation and putting forward my own positive suggestions, I need to clarify the terms used. The meaning of the word 'monetarism' has changed considerably in the last decade. It was originally the word used to describe the specific proposition that control of the money supply was a necessary prelude to the control of inflation. It is now used to cover the gamut of economic policies followed by the Government since 1979. To prevent misunderstanding, let me state now that, in this chapter and elsewhere in the book, I use 'monetarism' purely in the sense that it is popularly understood: as the total economic policy of the present Government. Similarly, the word 'monetarist' refers to the enthusiasts for the Government's economic policy, not to the original proponents of monetary theory. To make this clear, I have used these words between inverted commas throughout.

As it came to be understood, 'monetarism' can be explained in five propositions:

1. The greatest economic evil is inflation, because it increases the price of goods without increasing their value, thus reducing productivity and competitiveness and destroying jobs.

2. If the money supply is controlled, the money for excessive wage increases will not exist, except at the expense of someone else's job, because only a finite amount of money will exist at any time. 'One man's wage increase is another man's job.'

3. Another pressure on the money supply is excessive public borrowing. The gap between Government income and expenditure must be reduced. Since it is wrong to put up taxes, it is necessary to cut public spending.

4. This reduction in Government expenditure will enable taxation to be reduced, thus giving more incentive to industry and, along with the other benefits above, making the economy more competitive, helping it to grow and ensuring that ir provides secure jobs for the future.

5. These benefits will arise only if industry is allowed to operate without Government interference and in accordance with the demands of the market. Subsidies should be eliminated wherever possible, so that all businesses can find their true economic level.

These five propositions are essentially a set of value judgments. Most of them might be thought reasonable in many circumstances, but that does not mean that they constitute an economic policy. What transmuted this pot-pourri of propositions into what we now know as 'monetarism' was the insistence on regarding them as an all-embracing solution to every problem and as a universal doctrine of cause and effect. In this way, 'monetarism' was elevated from one specific proposition to an edifice of economic and industrial theory.

Today, 'monetarism' is no longer a fashionable word. Once it was impossible to read a newspaper or watch a current affairs programme without hearing it bandied about in a debonair fashion. Now it has been consigned to the addendum of the political dictionary, along with its appendages. M1, M2 and M3 have resumed their traditional role as means of reaching London; they are no longer touted as the means of reaching the first three stages of economic nirvana.

But, even if the word is now seldom used, the five propositions remain central to Government thinking. There has been no substantial slippage in policy. It is true that, in certain limited areas, economic policy has abandoned the icier frontiers of 'monetarism'. It is true that some disobliging features of the real world are necessitating a reappraisal of some aspects of the theory. It is clear that strict adherence to the creed is weakening. Noises are made that church and state might even separate at some point. But the fact remains that 'monetarism' was the starting point for Government policy; it has defined the approach to all important areas of economic policy; it remains the cornerstone of economic strategy and it is still held to be the true faith. Occasional lapses are reluctantly allowed, but they are never admitted.

I have always had doubts about 'monetarism', and I have steadily become a heretic. My doubt was due to my distrust of all rigid policies that are claimed to solve every problem, as I have never yet encountered one that actually does so. My heresy grew with the belief that, especially since the start of the recession, 'monetarism' provided an inadequate remedy for Britain's economic problems and was in many respects positively harmful.

Before discussing an alternative, the existing policy should be evaluated against its own criteria. The high priests of 'monetarism' declared that inflation would fall to almost nothing, productivity and competitiveness would increase, strong and well-founded growth would return to the economy and unemployment – already very high in 1979 – would gradually, if slowly, disappear. The dawn of a new golden age of prosperity was heralded. The advocates of 'monetarism' were quite certain as to its consequences and should not complain if they are now confronted with them, five years into the experiment.

Inflation soared initially, due partly to the increase in VAT but mainly to the legacy of the preceding Labour Government (notably the recommendations of the Clegg Committee on public sector pay awards), but then fell dramatically and has settled at a level of around five per cent. It is still higher than in many other industrialised countries which have not followed 'monetarist' policies.

Money supply has habitually exceeded its intended limits, which is perhaps why we hear less about it these days. After five years, there are still doubts as to whether and how it can be accurately measured.

Interest rates soared initially and are still very high, although they are gradually falling.

Wage increases still exceed growth in the GDP. For a long time, the country suffered from the failure of 'monetarists' to recognise that public sector wage increases could not be restrained in the same way that the theory predicted would happen in the private sector.

Exchange rates are now at a more realistic level, but for a long time sterling was greatly over-valued. This perhaps did as much as anything to accelerate industrial decline.

Productivity has improved, largely as the side-effect of unemployment, but less substantially than in several other industrialised countries, so the gap has increased and competitiveness has actually deteriorated.

Economic growth has returned only recently. Its long term reliability is not yet proven. It is based more on a small consumer-led boom than on an upsurge in industrial production. Much of our manufacturing base has disappeared in the last five years – perhaps around twenty-five per cent. We may now have higher growth than any other EEC country, but since we fell further than others, we need to rise further just to stand still.

Unemployment has climbed rapidly, although it has now stabilised at around three million on official statistics, which if anything understate the figures. Many people, myself included, believe that on present policies it will start climbing again.

Government expenditure has not only increased in real terms, but has risen as a percentage of the GDP.

Government borrowing has been reduced, but not as much as the Chancellor claims. As the House of Commons Select Committee has made clear, the figures have been slanted by treating the sale of fixed assets from the privatisation programme as current revenue, thus artificially reducing the Public Sector Borrowing Requirement.

Taxation has increased overall in personal terms, although income tax has been reduced and further reductions have been promised.

Subsidies to industry have been reduced recently and most of the nationalised industries are now more efficient than they were. They are also a lot smaller. The improvements were achieved only after substantial Government cash injections.

Overall the results are not especially impressive. Judged by the exacting standards of the 'monetarists', not a single objective has been completely achieved. My own verdict is less harsh than theirs ought to be. There are several mitigating factors. The legacy of years of failure to tackle some of the problems meant that overnight success was never possible. The effects of the world recession would have depressed growth and increased unemployment under any policies. Comparisons with other countries are often misleading, as statistics are available to support almost any point of view, and the situation elsewhere never truly reflects that at home. Finally, it must be stressed that the over-riding objective of 'monetarism' – the control of inflation – has been more nearly achieved than most other objectives.

But even if one allows for these factors, and even if one believes – as I do – that the picture would have been far bleaker under a Labour Government, one cannot conclude that 'monetarism' has been the saviour of the economy, nor even that it has tended to have the consequences that its advocates predicted. Not only are the achievements not there, but many of the trends are not there either.

Despite this, many people believe that, over the last few years, industry has become tougher in its attitudes, more determined in its outlook and more modern in its equipment and its methods, and that this is somehow the real victory of 'monetarism'. These things have indeed happened, but the improvements have had nothing to do with 'monetarism'. They are partly due to industrial trends that are unrelated to economic policy, but mainly to the harsh realities of the recession. Industry has been faced with adversity and has needed to respond. The Government's contribution to this process has been to give much needed moral support to industry: the only contribution of 'monetarism' has been to deepen the adversity.

In short, the Government has not understood the effect of 'monetarism' on industry. Visible economic gains divert attention from industrial decline. Lower inflation benefits everyone, whereas industrial decay and unemployment affect a minority in the short term. However, in the long term, they affect the whole country. The fallacy is to believe that 'monetarism' may have caused short term difficulties, but has won a long term gain. The evidence so far is that the only long term gain from 'monetarism' is to the dole queue. The new-found toughness derives almost entirely from the recession.

To explain the limitations of 'monetarism', one must consider both the theory and the practice. The theory is not entirely false, but neither is it universally true. The assumption of 'monetarism' is that inflation is the greatest economic evil. The first tenet of 'monetarism' – and its original source – is that control of the money supply will help to prevent inflation. I largely agree with the tenet: control of the money supply does contribute to low inflation. That is why the Government has been more successful in this respect than in meeting its other objectives, which are less tangibly related to the money supply. However, the error of 'monetarism' lies in its assumption, which is contentious on two counts.

The first is that, because 'monetarism' is a theory that deals primarily with inflation, it is not well-equipped to deal either with economic growth or with unemployment. In the right circumstances, successful control of inflation by 'monetary' methods may well help other economic objectives to be achieved. In the wrong circumstances, and without further measures being adopted, it tends to have an opposite effect.

This leads to the second problem. Inflation is no longer the major evil. Control of inflation is always important, but its importance relative to other factors will vary according to circumstances. When 'monetarism' became fashionable in the early 1970s, there was growth in the economy, unemployment was relatively low and the main problems were inflation and its corollary, reduced competitiveness. By the mid 1970s, when 'monetarism' was adopted as Conservative policy, the same was true, only more so. By early 1979 and at the time of the election, the diagnosis was still broadly correct, although unemployment had already increased considerably.

But the world recession changed the picture. The implementation of strict 'monetary' policies during a time of recession aggravated the difficulties. They still served to control inflation, but the consequences were a steep rise in unemployment, a disincentive to growth and the erosion of our industrial base. As a result, these problems are now so severe that they contradict the notion that helped to cause them – that inflation is the major problem.

It is on these grounds that I dispute the theory of 'monetarism'. It asserts propositions which may be true in some circumstances and pretends they are true in all circumstances. A set of opinions that were more or less sustainable in the mid-1970s has been turned into a universal truth. 'Monetarism' is founded on fixed and absolute assumptions in a world that is variable and relative. If one applies a fixed policy in a variable world, its effects will be variable. Such a policy cannot accommodate complexity and change.

Because 'monetarism' is inflexible theory, it has become bad practice. Above all, it has undermined its own objectives. Among the consequences of the recession that 'monetarism' has exacerbated, much the most serious is unemployment. There are now more than three million people who could be contributing to our industrial wealth but cannot do so. Apart from the sheer waste of it, this constitutes a vast drain on the Government's resources. Every 190,000 people on the dole queue represents at least one per cent of central Government expenditure in direct payments and lost revenue, leaving aside increased administrative costs. All three million represent about seventeen per cent of Government spending. This accounts for more expenditure than any other single area and, to give some perspective, more than housing, transport, agriculture and law and order put together.

'Monetarism' has inspired its own cycle of decline. Under the conditions of a world recession, 'monetary' policies have ensured that companies are more likely to contract or to collapse. This has produced a higher level of unemployment. This has increased the cost of social benefits. This has prevented total Government expenditure being cut, and has put pressure on all other areas of spending. This has made it impossible to cut taxes, and has forced severe cuts in capital expenditure. This has brought about further contraction. And so it goes on. For possibly the first time in history, the TUC and the CBI have been calling for almost the same remedial action for most of the last five years. The Government might at least have wondered what crisis prompted such an otherwise welcome event.

The economic cycle of decline has produced a social cycle of despair in many parts of the country. Because unemployment is so high and the cost of supporting it so great, the Government has been forced to restrict social security payments and other social spending. The result is that, while those in work get richer year by year, those out of work get relatively poorer. The unemployed are thus penalised twice: once by losing their jobs and again by seeing their living standards deteriorate. There is nothing that most of them can do to break this cycle. The two nations of modern Britain are the employed and the unemployed. They are growing further apart. The unemployed, however many, will always be in a minority, and thus tend to be disregarded by Governments that calculate an appeal to the material values of the majority.

To this catalogue of failure, there has been one reply: 'There is no alternative.' That is simply not true. There are always several alternatives. The starting point for mine is to desist from turning any theory into dogma. The need is for a policy that reflects a sensible balance of all the factors, not an ideology that is so bound up with one factor that it distorts the others. The change of viewpoint required is to stop seeing every issue in black and white and to acknowledge the gradation of greys that is reality. It is necessary to dispense with false antitheses, which have become so much part and parcel of 'monetarist' doctrine that we have come almost unthinkingly to accept them. We must start the thinking process again and should begin by taking a large eraser to rub out the hard and fast dividing lines that have been drawn. In particular, there are three such lines to eradicate:

- the division between 'real' jobs and 'false' jobs;

- the division between 'prudent' housekeeping and 'wicked' borrowing;

- the division between 'sensible' Government encouragement of industry and 'harmful' intervention.

There is no absolute distinction between 'real' and 'false' jobs.

Whenever anyone suggests the use of Government money to create more jobs, the response is that these would be 'false' jobs, because they would exist only through subsidy. When the Government pumped in billions of pounds to cover the losses of the nationalised industries, it was – by its own definition – perpetuating 'false' jobs. Several of those industries are now profitable. The jobs they provide have now become 'real' jobs. If 'false' jobs had not been protected, the 'real' jobs would not have materialised. So where is the dividing line?

In reality, all jobs are on a sliding scale of viability. In a company that sold nothing at all, all jobs would be one hundred per cent subsidised, in the unlikely event of their existing at all. In a highly successful company, the cost of each job would be recovered several times over. However, the majority of jobs hover within roughly a ten per cent margin of break-even either way. At any one time in any one company there is an absolute dividing line between profit and loss, but that line can vary substantially over time and is dependent on several factors outside the company's direct control. Many companies, or divisions of companies, will dip below the dividing line from time to time. If, every time they do so, the jobs involved are declared to be 'false' jobs and are not protected, the result will be a constant erosion of jobs. The conclusion of this process would be that the only jobs remaining would be with companies that never, under any circumstances, crossed the dividing line. This might indeed be the ideal, but it is hardly realistic.

Obviously one cannot subsidise every job indiscriminately, so let us consider what a competent businessman would do. He would look at the underlying viability of a division or a company. If he concluded that it was potentially viable, he would decide what action was needed and would then implement it. That might involve some redundancies, but it would not involve either closing the business or expecting it to be profitable from the start of its new operation. Few companies expect an immediate profit from a new venture and, in many industries, the profit is not expected for several years. A good businessman would assess the chances of an acceptable return in an acceptable timescale. Above all, he would want to find the means for future success, and not be resigned to denying it.

This, in fact, is exactly what the Government did with industries like the British Steel Corporation. The need for a streamlining of the industry was recognised. The money was put in. The management and workforce of BSC are now vindicating both the confidence and the investment. But this has tended to happen only in the largest and most visible industries, where collapse would have been politically disastrous. It has not happened in a sustained or widespread manner, or in the context of an overall industrial strategy.

Borrowing is not wicked and there is no perfect level for the Public Sector Borrowing Requirement.

Over the last five years, the Government has argued that to exceed its intended borrowing limits by the merest fraction would ruin its entire strategy. This is nonsense. Of course the line has to be drawn every year and, once drawn, it has to be defended. But there is no absolute veracity attached to it. One cannot argue that a pound either way invalidates everything, or assume that even several billion pounds either way would make an enormous difference. Nor can one view this one factor in isolation.

Over the years, Britain has not become prosperous through a reluctance to borrow. The twin strengths of capitalism are its responsiveness to market needs and its readiness to provide capital for long term investment. The Government rightly condemns state monopolies for destroying the first strength, but the removal of the second is equally debilitating. The flexibility of industry in its attitude to borrowing and to finance generally contrasts with the rigidity of the Government. Not only is borrowing deprecated, but there is a Micawber-like attitude to money in all its forms. In the modern world, money is not always a tangible commodity. Individuals spend money they do not have through credit cards, bank overdrafts and mortgages. Industry spends money it does not have by borrowing from banks and institutions. It is true there is always a lender – someone who does have the money – but that lender need not be based in Britain, nor does the money advanced need to be British money. There is therefore no finite amount of money available to this country, and borrowing more does not have to involve printing more, although it might well involve higher interest rates.

One's attitude to borrowing must depend on how the money is used. It might not matter to my bank balance today whether I borrow £500 to spend on a holiday or to invest on the stock market, but it matters greatly to how it might look in the future. As with industry, it depends on the wisdom of the investment.

Let us consider the response of a Government to the problem of a large industrial concern that employs 80,000 people, has a turnover of £750 million and is losing money. There is a choice between letting it crash and restructuring it. Let us suppose that the restructuring requires an immediate cash injection of £300 million to cover current losses and new investment, an allowance for losses of £100 million and £50 million in the next two years before break-even is achieved and a cut in the workforce from 80,000 to 50,000. The total cost over three years, including the cost of another 30,000 unemployed, would be about £900 million. 'What an appalling waste of money,' one might say, and no doubt 'monetarists' would. But the other alternative would cost the Government about £1,200 million over the same period and there would be nothing left to show for it at the end except the prospect of supporting 80,000 people to do nothing.

'Monetary' purists would argue that this is false logic, since the 80,000 people working in an unprofitable business would become available to work in a profitable one. That is some joke at present.

There are three million people unable to find a job in any business, profitable or not. This shows how different circumstances affect theories in different ways. If there was full employment and an unfilled demand for labour, the 'monetarist' argument might have more validity. In those circumstances, by all means let unprofitable businesses go to the wall and be replaced by profitable ones. But if there is a huge labour surplus, the policy becomes untenable.

If it is so simple, why is it not universally recognised? It is not that simple. The figures quoted in the example above conceal one other important fact: in the first year of the three year plan, the restructuring option would cost more than letting the company go under, about £50 million more in this case. Therefore, one might think, total Government expenditure would be increased in that year, with all the problems that entails.

But need this actually happen? I think we are too inclined to view the options as all or nothing: either the Government subsidises the entire operation, or it crashes. The Government does not need to take all the risk. If the company in question was privately owned, the immediate decision would be faced by its bankers. They might conclude that £900 million was an unacceptable risk. But, if the Government guaranteed part of that sum – and perhaps only a small part in some cases – that could change the bankers' perception of the risk. That is why the first requirement in industrial affairs is to be flexible enough to consider all the options. The second requirement is a preparedness to take a long term view. Investment implies investment in the future: it is not, and never can be, a short term process.

If operated sensibly, such a policy need not increase inflation. Other countries, and Britain at other times, have had low inflation without 'monetarist' policies. What matters is the correlation between growth and earnings, and between growth and non-productive expenditure. That is why growth is so vital and stagnation or decline so disastrous. We have seen the harmful side-effects of a growth-dominated strategy in the past, but that is no reason to cast growth aside and make it in turn a side-effect of something even less important.

Government intervention in industry is not necessarily bad and it is not necessarily good.

It depends on the way in which the Government intervenes and not on the fact of intervention. If Governments intervene to suppress the mechanism of the market, if they intervene to create monopolies and then think they know how to run them, if they intervene to remove from management and unions the power to reach their own decisions, the intervention is frequently calamitous. This is the type of intervention that prevailed through most of the 1960s and 1970s and was the cause of much of the grief that ensued.

The Government has rightly stopped the abuses of intervention. It has privatised state industries where possible and brought in first-rate industrialists to manage some of the remaining nationalised enterprises. It has banished the absurdity of midnight meetings over tea and sandwiches in Downing Street between management, unions and Prime Minister, reaching agreements that achieved only a specious political kudos. The smoke-filled rooms have gone and a breath of fresh air has come in their wake.

However, the objective cannot be merely to stop the abuses: a positive Government role must be constructed. It is not enough to stand on the touch-line and cheer loudly. The modern world is too complex, and many of the issues too pervasive, for industry to manage entirely on its own. The Governments of other countries are closely involved with their industries and often subsidise products in a way that distorts the free market, thus creating problems for British industry that are unrelated to objective competitiveness. This involvement has implications for us that only the Government can resolve. It must do so in partnership with British industry, and in the light of discussions with other Governments, notably in Common Market countries, the USA and Japan. Purists will say that such action tampers with the market, but the market is already tampered with by others and, if this fact of life is ignored, we will be the ones who suffer most.

The major change I would like to see in Government policy is the establishment of a coherent industrial strategy, which should include the creation of a partnership between Government, industrial management and unions. After five years, no such strategy exists. When I became Leader of the House of Commons in January 1981, I asked Keith Joseph, the Secretary of State for Industry, for a brief on his industrial strategy, only to be told that there was none. I suppose this was at least a step forward from his original strategy, which was to abolish his own Ministry, but it was still a disarming reply. Nothing much has changed since then.

The glaring gap in industrial policy – and the reason it does not amount to a strategy – is the absence of a sustained approach to existing businesses. The Government has given substantial assistance to new technology and to the establishment of new businesses, which I welcome, but in saying that these businesses represent our future it states a partial truth. Our future depends equally, in fact considerably more in the medium term, on how our existing industries develop and grow. The Government's attitude implies that these businesses should be left to sink or swim, while all the help is channelled into new industries. Sometimes one is inclined to think that it would like to tear everything down and start again.

An industrial strategy is needed that embraces the whole of British industry, and not just its newest sector. Investment also needs to be broader, and the Government should be involved in its co-ordination. There are many ways in which this could happen without spending huge sums of public money. One way would be to extend the existing policy of helping with finance for new businesses, whereby capital is raised through the banks, but most of it is guaranteed by the Government. The same policy could be applied to existing businesses and other financial institutions, without the Government underwriting the whole amount, or even most of it.

The strategy should incorporate practical policies to reduce unemployment. This need not involve spending more to create jobs than to maintain their absence. It now costs at least £5,000 a year on average to keep each person out of work. There is no reason why, at least as a temporary measure, the Government should not help to finance new jobs in the private sector – as it already does in some limited instances – and to save money by doing so. There are several options on both employment and investment, if one is flexible enough to consider them.

This new strategy must also include the creation of an industrial partnership, where the Government's role is supportive and strategic rather than coercive and operational. The roles of all three prospective partners were inadequate for too long. Governments intervened too much and in the wrong places. Managements often lacked courage, initiative and the spirit of partnership. Union leaders became the swaggering industrial power-brokers of the nation, with more authority larded out to them year by year and with no accountability required. All this has changed in the last five years. Government has withdrawn from over-interference. Managements have been obliged to face their responsibilities. Unions have been prevented from exercising their irresponsibility. This has resulted partly from the recession and partly from the tough line pursued by the Government. The time has come for the success to be consolidated.

The role of the unions and the way the Government approaches them will be vital. Until now, the Government's main aim has been to stop the abuse of union power. In the process, many union leaders have come to appreciate three facts. First, they recognise that their former role was unpopular in the country at large and even amongst their own members. Second, they know that in the long run they can ignore neither the economic facts of life, nor the application of new technology. Third, they have come to realise that their close identification with the Labour Party has damaged their reputation and has prevented them from being seen to act objectively in their members' interests.

Taking these three factors together, the opportunity exists for a fresh approach. It will not be easy. Many union leaders still repudiate the new realism emerging from their colleagues. Even the supporters of a new approach have deep misgivings about the Government. However much they accept both the potential benefits and the inevitability of new technology, it is hard for them to welcome it when its immediate effects are to lengthen the dole queue and often to weaken the position of their own unions. They also remain suspicious of the Government's objectives, let alone its policies, particularly where social service expenditure, industrial investment and further union legislation are concerned. At the same time, the Government will be suspicious as to the motives of the union leaders and will fear an attempt to regain their previous hegemony through the back-door.

There are therefore many obstacles to progress. However, decisive action now to tackle them could realise an opportunity that might not recur. It might seem paradoxical, but it would be in line with the best Tory tradition for the Conservative Party to take the lead in helping the unions towards a new and more constructive role. If it did so successfully, it could change the political as well as the industrial landscape. I hope the Government has the sense to recognise this opportunity, although the handling of the GCHQ dispute does not inspire confidence that it yet has.

If there is one feature that unites the most successful economies in the world it is stability: not in the sense of a soporific immovability, but of a clear identity of interest between Government, industry and unions as to their respective roles and responsibilities, where all are partners working to the same end. Since the war, Britain has rarely enjoyed such stability, and this is perhaps the major cause of our steady economic decline. The so-called British consensus was a mutual agreement by all concerned to differ on these issues. If this is the consensus the Government wishes to break, I am all for it – as long as the creation of a new consensus, which is genuinely shared by the nation, is the end in view.

*

In the course of this chapter, I have outlined the inadequacy of 'monetarism' in the context of the alternative approach that I would prefer. I must restate that, while I believe 'monetarism' has exacerbated many problems, those problems would have existed anyway in the wake of the world recession and many have been endemic to our economy for far longer than that. The policies advocated by the Labour Party at the 1983 election would not have solved the difficulties and would have made them worse in the long term. But that is still no excuse for 'monetarism'.

There is never only one approach. Alternatives always exist. The failure of 'non-monetarist' Conservatives is not that we have lacked a realistic alternative, but that we have not articulated it with sufficient vigour and clarity. The strength of our approach is that it is unencumbered with dogma, which is also its weakness. It is easier to understand a fixed assertion than an approach that is not fixed and is open to individual interpretation. Many people who are not Socialists have consistently argued against 'monetarist' policies. But we have been a disparate, unorganised group, lacking both an identity and clearly-perceived policies. If we are now being proved right, it has more to do with reality making our case for us than with us having successfully made it on our own behalf.

In the hope that it might now be taken seriously, let me end by summarising the direction I would like economic policy to take, and have argued that it should have taken ever since the advent of the recession called into question both the hypothesis and the effects of strict 'monetarism'.

First, the objective of creating sustained non-inflationary growth must be maintained, but the approach to achieving it should involve a balanced view of all factors – notably growth, unemployment and inflation – not an over-emphasis on one factor that distorts the rest.

Second, much more industrial investment is required. As part of this, the Government must be prepared to spend and to borrow more than at present to enable regeneration to take place. It should be done sensibly and gradually, but those who argue that it should not be done at all need constantly to be reminded that unemployment already costs the Exchequer at least £15 billion a year and produces nothing in return.

Third, the Government must develop an industrial strategy that encompasses growth, investment, employment and a response to foreign competition, and that covers industry as a whole and not just the new sectors. In doing so, it must make it plain that investment funding does not mean open-ended financial commitment and will be made only in the context of a viable business plan and with an agreement to realistic manning levels. The motive is financial: a reduction in unemployment should be seen as the consequence of investment, not a self-sufficient justification for it.

Fourth, the Government should build a partnership with management and unions, with its own role being supportive rather than intrusive. If it does so in the context of the other recommended policies, I believe that union leaders will be more co-operative over both manning levels and the introduction of new technology.

Fifth, the whole approach needs to become more flexible. This does not equate to weakness and expediency. The need is for a firm perseverance towards the objectives in a way that takes account of changing circumstances. Success is threatened, not only by expediency, but by inflexibility.

Sixth, if the above policies are implemented, it is my belief that inflation will continue to be contained. Nothing I have suggested involves either a substantial increase in current Government expenditure, or unjustified wage increases, or permanent Government subsidies to unviable businesses. I do not want to undermine the Government's economic achievements, but to extend them. Everything is related to profitable growth achieved through considered investment and an industrial partnership.

These policies will not solve the problems overnight. Nothing has and nothing will. The road to recovery will be slow and steady. What matters is that it is the right road, and that it is built on real terrain and not on the abstract landscape of an arid ideology.

NINE

After the Recession

'Increased means and increased leisure are the two civilisers of man.' – DISRAELI

'It is probable that when the history of the present period comes to be written, it will be seen as a hiatus between the old economic system and the new. It is a period which cannot yet be dignified by the name transition. For to visualise a transition it is necessary to see more or less clearly both the beginning and the end of the process. The history of events has made us familiar with the framework of the system which we are leaving behind. Unfortunately there is no such clarity about our destination. Nor is social inventiveness even keeping pace with the pressure of events. The great need of the moment is not only for a policy of action to deal with a pressing situation, but for a new theory of social and economic organisation which will facilitate the evolution towards a new economic system suitable to the changed circumstances of the modern world . . .

'. . . There is a need for a mobilisation of all the moderate and intelligent elements in the country who are not misled by temporary indications that everything will come right of its own accord. These elements are sufficiently numerous to ensure that the drastic changes which are seen to be essential when the real nature of the crisis is understood, are carried out with courage and with expedition . . . (The requirement is for) constructive proposals which appeal to the reason and intelligence of the nation, and which can be shown both in argument and in practice to be adequate for the creation of a system in which we shall be able to enjoy the fruits of increased productivity made possible by the bounty of nature and the applied genius of mankind.'

These words were written by Harold Macmillan in 1933. The circumstances in which he wrote them were in many respects different from those of today. The Depression of the 1930s cut deeper than our present recession; the human and social consequences were worse; the rise of totalitarianism in Russia, Italy and Germany threatened our own democracy; the prospects for future prosperity seemed less favourable than they do today. Yet the 1930s contained the seeds of a change that was both deep and limitlessly pervasive in its effect upon our economy and our society, as do the 1980s. That is why Harold Macmillan's plea from fifty years ago rings such loud bells today.

In the 1930s, the challenge was to move from uninhibited free market capitalism to welfare capitalism, while coping with the legacy of the Depression, the decline in many of Britain's traditional industries and profound changes in the pattern of world trade. In the 1980s and beyond, the challenge is to move from highly mechanised – but still labour-intensive industries – to technology-intensive industries, while coping with the legacy of the recession, the further decline in many of Britain's traditional industries and new changes in the pattern of world trade. In doing so, the difficulties are perhaps even greater in the social than in the economic area, as they also were in the 1930s. Social patterns tend to follow economic patterns. But, while economic patterns respond quickly to the imperatives of reality, social patterns change more slowly and reluctantly. In any period of great change, the danger exists that the two elements will break step. Few things are more damaging to a nation than such an imbalance.

This chapter addresses that future. By its nature, it involves gazing into a crystal ball. It may therefore be wrong, as may everyone else's assessment. The one certainty in a period of great change is that many people living through it will misjudge its nature, its timing and its consequences. Such a thought should sober all of us, but discourage nobody. The alternative is to think nothing, say nothing, do nothing. Instead, the difficulty of forming a correct judgment argues the need for everyone to think about the issues and to debate them. In that way, a 'best guess' view can be reached, as opposed to the more limited view of a handful of people, who may prove to be spectacularly right but may equally well be spectacularly wrong.

I have called this chapter 'After the recession', because that is what it truly concerns. I want us to lift our heads above the parapet of our beleaguered garrison and look beyond the enemy at the gate. Such a title may seem to assume that the recession will shortly end, if it has not already done so. I do not make that assumption. We should all be heartened by recent signs of a modest recovery, but at present they are no more than that. There can be no certainty that the causes of recession have disappeared, let alone its effects. The size of the American budget deficit, its likely impact on Western interest rates, the scale of international indebtedness, the danger of economic collapse in South or Central America in particular, the threat to oil supplies of the Iran–Iraq War, the eventual exhaustion of our own oil reserves, and the major changes taking place in world trade as nations with lower living standards undercut the West, all serve as warnings of what could yet go wrong. Such danger signals always exist and often prove to be unfounded, as I hope these will do. But the Western economies, in starting to recover from a major illness, have a low resistance to new infections. One cannot assume that none of the dangers will materialise and that we are now on the road to full health. There are grounds for cautious optimism, but not for euphoria.

None of this obviates the need to consider the wider issues of the future, and in particular the economic and social impact of new technology. This impact will be substantial, whatever happens with the recession. It offers us a great opportunity, but it also presents great problems that will need to be solved if the opportunity is to be realised. The effects of the recession have already exacerbated these problems: whether it abates or continues will not determine the future opportunity created by new technology, but it will affect the scale of the problems that precede the opportunity.

Given the problems of the last decade, it is not surprising that our minds have been concentrated on the present: how do we cure inflation? how do we stop unemployment rising? how do we get growth back into the economy? Behind these questions is the largely unconsidered assumption that, once we climb out of the recession, life will be sweetness and light: we will be back to the heady days of the late 1950s and the 1960s, with full employment, rising living standards and a bonanza all round. But it will not be like that – at least not unless we pay attention to some new features of the modern world and find original political approaches to them.

Above all, there is one fallacy held about life after the recession, which is that when it ends and when sustained growth returns to the economy, there will be a steady if slow return to full employment. This will not happen. Indeed, it is feasible that unemployment could actually rise as the economy recovers. If gains in productivity outstrip economic growth, without a commensurate reduction in working hours, unemployment will be bound to rise. That is the first issue to consider. In doing so, I want to explain the historical factors behind it, to paint the picture of the future as I see it, to consider the implications of that future – economically, socially and politically – and to outline some necessary action.

Let me stress at the outset that I am not a prophet of doom. These changes represent one of the great opportunities of history – provided they are properly anticipated and are handled with imagination, foresight and sensitivity. It is only if they are not so handled that the potential for catastrophe will be revealed. The changes are best gathered under one phrase: 'the technological revolution'. To understand the roots of this revolution, we need to look at the last comparable stage of economic upheaval – the first industrial revolution.

Two main factors characterised this revolution. The first was the invention of machinery to replace many repetitive human functions. The second was the harnessing of energy resources to power that machinery. The consequence was a simple form of automation that allowed raw materials to be processed into finished goods more rapidly and in far greater quantity and quality than before. Because the automation was still basic, there remained a massive need for human labour. The role of man in this process was mechanistic: he was the link between machines, filling in the processes of production for which machines had not yet been developed.

This was indeed an industrial revolution. But it was every bit as much a social revolution, because it changed the face of British society. A predominantly rural society became a predominantly urban one. Where there was industry, there were jobs. Where there were jobs, there came people to fill them. Where there came people, there grew towns and cities. Even today, the population pattern is largely conditioned by the pattern of available employment from the early nineteenth century onwards.

Social historians and politicians have argued the consequences of this revolution since it began. Industrialisation required man to be a machine. It demanded work that was repetitive, unskilled and unthinking. It divorced the individual from the product he made and related him to a single process, which was in itself often meaningless to him. Such was the nature of industrial production and in many ways it remains so. In economic terms, labour became a component of production in the same way as capital, raw materials and machinery. In human terms, that was of course untenable and this conflict has been at the root of political debate ever since industrialisation.

But there was another side to the coin. Whatever the human evils of industrialisation, they were not always worse than they had been before. The myth persists of an agrarian golden age, with jolly peasants dancing round the village maypole. Life was never like that for most people. More to the point, the living standards we now enjoy – standards that were unimaginable for ninety per cent of the population even fifty years ago – are the product of industrialisation and could not have developed without it. The process, like many things in life, was a trade-off. The penalty was a long, hard working life of considerable tedium. The reward was a far better standard of living. The dominant motive became materialism. One can debate whether that has been an entirely healthy development, but it is a separate debate.

Material growth reached its peak through the 1960s. In retrospect, it is not hard to see that we took too much for granted at that time. We were prosperous, but progressively less prosperous than other nations. We were lagging in innovation, in investment, in productivity, in competitiveness. Our management was often bad, its methods outdated. We can see more clearly now why, when the tide did turn across the world, it turned on us with especial venom. But at the time, it seemed different. British industry still appeared to be in good shape: it held strong shares of most domestic markets and our role as a major exporting nation was sustained. There was a substantial increase in consumer demand across the world. This, together with the fact that most industries were still labour-intensive, meant that full employment could be maintained, despite the growth in population and despite the increase in the number of women in work. In 1950, there were 20.75 million people in full-time employment; in 1970 there were 22.5 million.

More demand. More jobs. More wealth. Those years now seem like a cornucopia of prosperity, and it is no wonder. But then the music stopped. The cycle of growth became a cycle of decline. The single factor that triggered the change was the sudden and huge increase in raw material costs, especially the first explosion in the price of oil in 1973. But we cannot blame everything on that. What really happened was that this one change exposed the other shortcomings in our economy that we had failed to mend during the good times. The increase in raw material costs meant that finished goods cost more to produce, so prices went up. In order to preserve the ever-rising living standards to which we had become accustomed as of right, we paid ourselves more than our output justified. Because national earnings exceeded the growth in national production, the consequence was further to increase the price of British goods. Our industry became less competitive: not only did this make it harder to sell our products in world markets, but it enabled other countries to sell their products more easily in Britain. This was the true meaning and effect of the inflationary spiral. We produced the same goods at a higher and higher price, and they became of poorer and poorer value.

The reversal of this destructive spiral necessarily became the first economic priority when Margaret Thatcher became Prime Minister. Had the spiral continued unchecked, as it looked like doing in the late 1970s, the effects would have been as devastating as anything we have yet witnessed. Recovery depended on two things: a curb on inflation and a growth in productivity. In that way, British goods would become of relatively better value and we would sell more. But, as the last chapter explained, the world recession added a new dimension to the problem. To improve productivity at a time of growing demand means using the same number of people to produce more, but to improve it at a time of stagnant demand means using fewer people to produce the same. To improve it when demand is actually reduced has a still more drastic effect: hence the growth and the scale of unemployment.

Even if a sustained recovery out of recession is now achieved – which is by no means certain – we will be left with a vast unemployment problem, unless we plan different action now. This will be partly the result of the recession, partly of current economic policy, but also of the rapid acceleration of the technological revolution.

There is an orthodox explanation of how the recession will end and what will happen afterwards. It runs along these lines: 'British industry will become more competitive. Productivity is already rising. Wage increases are moderate. Prices are under control. We are increasingly able to offer good value products to home and overseas markets. As the worldwide recovery begins, there will be a renewed growth in demand, with Britain well placed to take an expanding share of it. At the same time, the Americans will control their budget deficit, interest rates will fall and this will aid investment for the future. The consequence is that British industry will sell more and more. It will need to produce more and more, so new jobs will be created and unemployment will be reduced. In short, we will return to the boom times of the 1960s, except without the endemic problems beneath the surface.'

This is an attractive scenario and one that it would be comforting to believe. But among its many assumptions (several of which are beyond the means of anyone in this country to influence, let alone control) is the cardinal assumption that a growth in output will create substantial new employment. In my opinion, that assumption is mistaken and should be reconsidered in the light of new technology.

Over recent years, new technology has come out of the science-fiction books into our lives. Yet do we realise quite what a dramatic revolution this is – a revolution to compare with the first industrial revolution? The advance in computers, in robotics, in micro-chip technology generally, has meant that human functions can be performed by machines in a way that is out of all proportion to previous mechanical developments. Earlier I described the human role in the industrial revolution as the link between machines. In the technological revolution, there is no link between machines. A fully-automated factory is what it says: fully-automated. And yet this is only part of it. Not only are more and more physical functions performed by technology, but what we used to think of as mental functions – functions of logic – are being performed by technology as well. Even the supervisory function is being eroded by technology, as equipment is developed that not only manufactures a product, but is able to diagnose faults in the materials or errors in the system. Motor car manufacturers who used to boast that a hundred people checked each car before it left the factory will soon boast that a hundred computers have checked it – or, more likely, one computer.

Who can doubt that this whole process, of which we are only now witnessing the beginning, will have the most profound influence on the working lives of everyone in this country, and indeed in the developed world? We are at the dawn of a change so momentous that it will force us completely to revise our traditional attitudes to employment and to how it is structured and organised.

In the light of these developments, we should reappraise the authorised version of what will happen after the recession. Under the revised version, even if the conditions are established that lead to sustained economic growth, the jobs will not automatically return – at least not in their old form. I refer specifically to manufacturing industry in this respect. Of course new jobs will be created in service industries, but in manufacturing industry – the historical backbone of our wealth and employment – the picture will be different. The traditional heavy industries, where so much of the burden of unemployment has fallen in the last few years, have shed hundreds of thousands of jobs which will not return when things get better. The industries to have survived will have done so by taking advantage of the new technology. Never again will their workforce be anything like its previous size. Furthermore, the new industries that have emerged and will emerge, will not be labour-intensive. They will not be able to absorb the high residual level of unemployment. The whole structure of industry will be different.

So far, I have described these changes on a broad scale. To give a more specific idea of the implications, let me express the point in terms of the working lives of ten average people. If we look back to 1968, a time of virtually full employment, those ten people would probably all have been in work. They would each have been working, on average, 45.8 hours a week, for 48.5 weeks a year and with the probability of doing so for 50 years, from 16 to 65. Between them, those ten people would have contributed 1.1 million working hours in their lives.

If we come forward fifteen years to 1983, of those ten people, at least one would have been out of work, as employment had fallen by nearly 10 per cent. That leaves nine full-time jobs. On average, those nine people would have worked shorter hours – about 42 hours a week, for 47.5 weeks a year, and still for 50 years. Between them, the ten people would have contributed just under 900,000 working hours in their lives, compared with 1.1 million in 1968. Yet they were then producing 22 per cent more than they did in 1968, so the hours required to generate the same output have been reduced by 33 per cent – by one third in fifteen years. And that is before we have experienced anything like the full impact of the new technology.

If we move forward another fifteen years to 1998, I do not find it far-fetched to imagine that the same output will be achieved in half the number of hours that it took in 1983. If we apply our current assumptions about employment (42 hours a week for 47.5 weeks for 50 years), by the end of the century we will need only four or five of those ten people to do the work of all of them.

The immediate riposte is that this argument is invalid as it is based on zero growth, whereas the strategy depends on creating growth. But such a riposte again fails to appreciate the nature of these changes. Previously, if a company's output rose by 10 per cent, one would expect its manpower requirements to rise by nearly the same amount – perhaps by 7 or 8 per cent. But in companies that are technology-intensive rather than labour-intensive, manpower requirements will be less directly related to variations in output. It is not unreasonable to assume that an average output increase of 10 per cent will require an average labour increase of only 4 per cent. If this ratio is roughly correct, economic growth will not fill the employment gap. If the economy grows in real terms by 3 per cent a year over the next fifteen years, that would amount to a compound growth of 56 per cent over the period – two and a half times the rate we have achieved in the last fifteen years. Under my assumption, this growth would be absorbed by an employment gain of only 22 per cent on the new low base.

If we return to those ten people, that means that by 1998 only four or five will be needed to service current output, and one more to service growth at the rate of 3 per cent a year. We would require growth of more than 20 per cent a year to hold unemployment at its current level and of more than 25 per cent to secure full employment. Under these circumstances, normal economic growth cannot cure unemployment.

I must stress that these comments refer only to manufacturing industry, which already represents a fairly small proportion of total employment. I do not suggest that half the country will be out of work by the end of the century. Two other factors will mitigate the picture I have painted: a compensating rise in employment opportunities in service businesses, and a continued slow reduction in working hours in manufacturing industry. Both these things will happen to some extent: the question is whether they will happen to a sufficient extent to secure an eventual return to more or less full employment. The Government thinks they will, but I do not.

New technology does not intrinsically create a growth in service industries, merely the opportunity for such growth. For the opportunity to be realised, there needs to be substantial economic growth. Services cannot be provided unless people can pay for them and nobody, whether individuals or businesses, will be able to pay for them without economic growth and a consequent rise in disposable income. It is fallacious to attribute the growth of service industries over the last twenty years to the growth of new technology. It should be attributed to a rise in disposable income. Nor should we forget that much of this development was false itself: if disposable income had not exceeded real growth over most of the period, there would be fewer service industries and more competitive manufacturing industries today.

If one accepts the correlation between disposable income and service industry employment, one can make some educated guesses about future prospects. Between 1961 and 1983, real disposable income rose – for the average person – by 62 per cent, and employment in service industries by 30 per cent. Translating this into the future, let us again assume an optimistic 3 per cent annual growth rate (56 per cent by 1998) and, in line with Government policy, that disposable income will rise by the same amount and no more. On these assumptions, there will be a 27 per cent increase in service industry employment over the period, representing 3.5 million additional jobs.

Before we throw our hats in the air in jubilation, we should pause to consider three further facts. First, the number of people of working age will have increased by 0.6 million by 1998. Second, if new technology has the effect on manufacturing industry that I have suggested, by 1998 the country will have to cope with a further 2.5 million or so unemployed, in addition to the current figure of more than 3 million. Taking all these factors into account, there would still be at least 2.6 million people out of work. Third, if instead of achieving a 56 per cent growth over the next fifteen years we achieve only the 22 per cent growth we have achieved in the last fifteen years, unemployment will be around 4.7 million – nearly double the number of people who, by that time, will remain in manufacturing industry. All these points underline the extent to which continued recession affects the scale of future problems, as well as the folly of assuming that the recession is now over.

In the light of this, it is not unduly pessimistic to anticipate unemployment of between 2.5 and 4.5 million from now until the end of the century and beyond, even after an allowance is made for the growth in service industries. If this is true, a continued slow reduction in working hours will make an insufficient impact on the problem. If the rate of the last fifteen years is maintained, it will reduce unemployment roughly to between 2 million and 4 million.

I do not present these figures as a prediction of what will happen, but as an indication of what well might. They amount to a speculation based on existing knowledge. I have not been pessimistic in my assumptions: if I have erred at all, I would expect it to be on the side of optimism. The low threshold assumes a high and sustained level of growth and a ready transfer of employment into service industries, both doubtful propositions. There are several factors, especially those that threaten recovery from recession, that could push the figure above the top threshold. Some industrialists expect unemployment to reach 9 million by the end of the century. I do not agree with them, but their opinions do not encourage the view that the problem will disappear altogether.

We cannot ignore what has happened in the last fifteen years. Despite economic growth of 22 per cent, despite a 10 per cent fall in the number of working hours in the year, despite a consistent growth in service industries, total employment has fallen by nearly 10 per cent. And we have witnessed only the beginning of the effect of new technology. Normal increases in economic growth will be insufficient to contain this effect, as it gathers pace in the future.

I have used specific figures so that the issues can be more clearly understood. They are soundly based, but they should not be taken literally. No one can apply an exact science to the future. The reality will be more diverse than the one I have portrayed and will contain elements that have occurred to nobody. I am merely trying to paint the picture of the way things are going, so that we can all appreciate the magnitude of the changes and the scale of the problem. Above all, I want to convince people that, even if we continue gradually to reduce working hours and even if growth accelerates over the coming years, we will still have dramatically high unemployment unless we consider the question in a different way. Yet, far from being a pessimist, I insist that this presents an opportunity as well as a problem. It depends entirely on how we approach it. If we think of it as 'unemployment in manufacturing industry is doubled', it is a *problem* of huge proportions. If we think of it as 'the working week is halved', it is an *opportunity* of huge proportions.

The core issue is not unemployment: it is the total number of working hours needed to produce what we can sell. Unemployment is only the expression of one particular way of dividing that total. These two issues have been confused, but they are not the same, and the key to resolving the problem and grasping the opportunity is to separate them. We should leave unemployment on one side for the moment and concentrate on how we approach the total number of working hours required. Considered in this way, a new issue of political economics is created.

At least since the birth of universal suffrage, political economics have principally concerned two factors: the creation of wealth and the distribution of wealth. The rival creeds of free enterprise and Socialism have disagreed about both and, more particularly, about the priority between the two. This is the battleground on which twentieth century politics have been fought, and it seems to me that free enterprise is close to having that battle won. People increasingly understand that free enterprise is more successful at creating wealth and that, unless wealth is created, social progress is impossible. Within this debate, unemployment has been an important factor, but the creation of employment has been largely linked to the creation of wealth. It is that link that will now be broken. If high economic growth no longer ensures or requires full employment, the two things become necessarily separate. Alongside the perennial factors of the creation and distribution of wealth is now a third major factor, which is most accurately described as the distribution of employment. We must change our attitudes to recognise that fact and what it means.

The first thing it means is that the two most prevalent philosophies to deal with unemployment – laissez-faire capitalism and Socialism – are both inadequate.

The laissez-faire orthodoxy holds that employment should be left to market forces. The consequence is that there is full-time employment for as many people as industry needs, with the balance of manpower being unemployed. This has the merit of promoting industrial competitiveness and can sometimes be justified in the short term on these grounds. However, unless economic growth eliminates unemployment – which it will not – this policy is untenable in the long term. It will produce a constantly high level of people permanently out of work. It will continue to attach a stigma to unemployment. It will divide the country between those who work and those who do not. It will be unacceptable economically, socially, politically and, I would add, morally too.

The Socialist orthodoxy is no more attractive. It seeks to provide full-time employment for everyone, under all circumstances. It does not fully accept the link between industrial efficiency on the one hand, and pay and employment on the other. It will depress productivity, perpetuate lack of competitiveness and lead to renewed inflation, without – I must stress – reducing unemployment in the long term.

However, there is a middle way, which depends on rejecting the traditional notions of employment. We are facing a reduction in the demand for labour in manufacturing industry. If we continue to allow this reduced demand to be expressed as unemployment, we will create permanent mass unemployment. If we allow it to be expressed as low productivity, we will create permanent lack of competitiveness. But, if we can assimilate the lower demand by reducing the number of hours worked by each individual in a working life, the reduction in labour can be spread evenly through society, without the stigma and futility of mass unemployment and without harming productivity or competitiveness. In selecting the variable factor in the supply mechanism that can accommodate changes in demand, we should reject both cost per unit and number of people employed, and choose instead the number of hours worked.

If, in fifteen years' time, we need half the working hours in manufacturing industry that we need now, this can be achieved in many other ways than by halving the working population. It can be achieved by a reduction in the working day, by a reduction in the working week, by longer holidays, by earlier retirement, by raising the age of entry into the labour market through longer training for young people – or, as is more likely, by a combination of all these things. If we can become less rigid in how we approach employment, we can find solutions that are a positive benefit to people. Thus the first implication of the technological revolution is the need for a change of attitude. The other implications are so widespread and profound that they deserve to be the subject of a book in their own right. Here, I can only summarise some of them briefly.

First, there are the educational implications. The advent of technology means that, not only will the demand for labour be reduced, but it will change in nature. Traditionally, a large percentage of employment in this country has been taken up by unskilled or semi-skilled labour. It is mainly this work that will be replaced by new technology. The jobs that remain will be more specialised and more skilled. This will require industrial training on a massive scale as well as a new approach to higher education. At present, there is a shortage of skilled labour in the industries where it is most needed. Without urgent action, the consequence will be an auction for those skills, which will in turn lead to higher industrial costs and renewed wage inflation.

Second, there are the social implications. I described earlier how the pattern of available employment since the industrial revolution had largely dictated population patterns. One distressing feature of the recession is that it has affected different communities in different ways, and the areas hardest hit have been those with the old labour-intensive industries. We need to consider whether the geographical pattern of future employment can match the pattern of past employment and, if not, what we are going to do about it. This will have a major bearing on both housing and industrial policy. Once the cities followed the jobs: is it now possible for jobs to follow the cities? The example of Government trying to encourage such a process in the late 1960s does not give grounds for optimism. But unless a way is found, the only alternative will be a major relocation of families, which in turn will have a radical effect on the infrastructure of the country.

Third, there are the implications for government spending and taxation. There will be an earlier retirement age, so pensions will become more costly. There will need to be a greater emphasis on technical and industrial training, so there will be a greater burden on education, even though the school population is now falling. There are already problems with the future funding of the health service. In real terms, there will need to be a significant growth in Government expenditure on the social services, which will require sustained economic growth to be affordable. Fewer people will pay tax, so each will pay more, and economic growth is again essential to make that possible without increasing the levels of taxation. Each of these areas will need the most careful consideration.

Fourth, there are the human implications of the changes. A reduction in the working life should be a great benefit to us all, but only if we find stimulating and satisfying things to do with our greater leisure time. The most challenging freedom is the choice of what to do with our time, as it forces us to rely on our inner resources, to use our time creatively and not to succumb to a life of boredom, inertia or, at worst, anti-social activity. The demands on education will therefore lead in two opposite directions. On the one hand, we shall need a more narrow and technical training. On the other hand, we shall need a broader education for a fuller life. We will need to face simultaneously the challenges of different work, increased leisure and, for many people, the prospect of pulling up roots and starting a new life. If the attitudinal change is the most pressing need, the human change has the most dramatic possibilities.

Finally, there are the political implications of this process. However great the sense of opportunity, there must be an equal sense of the inherent difficulties. Each individual aspect is a political challenge in its own right. When they are put together, the task is formidable. Much will depend on how the subject is presented to people and received by them. I would like to think that, where we now read 'unemployment at three million', in years to come we may read 'leisure time doubled for six million'. Indeed, instead of using the terms 'employment' and 'unemployment', we might gradually learn to talk about 'occupation' instead. That change would be the epitome of success, because we would have altered the entire way in which we think about our working lives. It will only be possible if we continue to create wealth. But if we do that, and if we then learn to share both employment and its rewards on an equitable basis, we have the makings of a different society. To fulfil that opportunity, three steps need to be taken.

First, we need to understand more precisely the nature of these changes and their likely effects. I am not an economist; still less am I a technologist. One does not have to be either to identify the changes and to understand some of their ramifications. But it will take people with these specialist skills fully to understand where the technological revolution is leading us.

Next, the whole issue must become a subject of public debate. Discussion should not be confined to private groups of specialists. Such profound social and economic changes should be the subject of a national debate, which the Government must lead. The media must also play their part: when I and others have tried to open the issue over the last few years, there has been a deafening silence from them in response.

Last, the Government should plan a concerted strategy that encompasses all the issues raised by the technological revolution. There may be grave suspicion of anything that smacks of economic interference or social planning, but some things are of too overwhelming and pervasive importance to be left to the natural ebb and flow of life. This is one of them.

As part of the process, the Government should work together with industry and the unions in planning a future strategy. Industry will understand the changes better than the Government, because it is through industry that they will happen. The process of adapting to these changes cannot take place without union involvement, in two areas in particular. The introduction of new technology will be further impeded if there is no union agreement to it. Second, a reduction in working hours cannot be allowed to impair competitiveness. We need to share the total available pay as well as the total required hours. People are unlikely to accept a wage reduction, but they might accept reduced hours in lieu of increased wages. This is understandably a current problem in industrial negotiations, although it is possible that many working people would be prepared to make sacrifices in this area, especially if it secured employment for their children, and also if the total earnings of the family were protected by having more of its members in work. In both areas, union co-operation is indispensable and will only be forthcoming if the Government mitigates the effects in other ways.

The Government also needs to discuss the issues with the other members of the European Community and with the Governments of other industrialised nations. We all face the same future, and its opportunities depend on us finding the best collective answer to the problems. The views and experience of other countries can help us, and we can help them. We do not have to sit in a corner, fearing that we are alone in our predicament. The same difficulties will be experienced throughout the world.

There are signs that the Government is starting to take some of the necessary action, but it has not gone far or fast enough and – more important – it still appears to lack an overall strategy. I am not sure that the Government even understands the nature and scale of some of the problems that it and its successors will face. In January 1984, Kenneth Baker, the Minister for Information Technology, made an important speech in which he addressed some of the issues that I and others had raised, and which I have described in this chapter. It is reasonable to assume that this speech represents Government policy on the technological revolution – nothing else has been said that contradicts it.

The speech makes two things clear: first, that the Government expects the technological revolution to have the same effects as I and most other people do and, second, that it sees no need to make special provision for these effects and believes that they will happen naturally and smoothly. There are references to a radical change in the working day, to a substantial increase in leisure time, to shifts in population patterns, to extensive retraining schemes etc. We share the same scenario. Thereafter, we differ on two points – the level of future unemployment and the need for further Government action. I have already explained my views on the first point, so let me examine the second. The speech acknowledges that 'attention is often focused on the first impact, when the greater volume of output as a result of increased productivity can lead to an employment loss', but expects this first impact to be short-lived. Inaction is not advised, but in saying that 'the Government must not be complacent; there are several things it must continue to do', the speech does not presage any new initiatives.

I am afraid that the tone of the speech suggests that the Government is indeed complacent, and that its policy is essentially one of laissez-faire in all areas except the important – but limited – one of assistance to high technology businesses. It acknowledges the parallel with the first industrial revolution, which it interprets in the following way: that it was only possible through the unshackled ability of industry to innovate, that it was accompanied by a passive Government role, that its effects were wholly beneficial and that the Jeremiahs of the time were wrong. The Government has then applied the same reasoning to the technological revolution, which is why, although it has some specific policies in the area, it has no overall strategy.

On the first point of interpretation, I agree that the unshackled ability of industry to innovate is vital to success. I wholeheartedly applaud what has been done in this area and the imagination that has been shown. The credit is due to the Government in general and to Kenneth Baker and his Department in particular. In fairness to him, I should add that my areas of criticism are not his responsibility.

On the second point, I do not agree that the role of Government during the industrial revolution was passive. On the contrary, it needed to become more and more active as time went on and as the economic and social consequences of the revolution became more severe. With the benefit of hindsight, we should conclude that, had Governments been able to anticipate the problems, they would have been able to prevent much hardship and misery.

On the third point, the effects of the industrial revolution were by no means wholly beneficial, at least not immediately so. Such a view telescopes history to an inordinate degree. For a long time after it had started, many of its supposed beneficiaries suffered reduced living standards. It took a long time for the benefits to be anything like universal, and for the other human and social problems to be tackled. This process should, I agree, be much quicker today, but it will still take a long time, especially if we again fail to anticipate the problems. It is unreasonable, and untenable politically, to tell people that they should not worry about the 'first impact' of unemployment and that history will prove their fears to be groundless. We have hopes for the future, but we live in the present. People will not readily accept an indefinite period of hardship for the sake of posterity, particularly when nothing appears to be done to acknowledge or to ameliorate it.

On the fourth point, I accept that the Jeremiahs were wrong, but only in respect of those who argued that industrialisation would be the ruination of the country. In that sense, I am not a Jeremiah now, nor is any sensible person. We all share the feeling of opportunity. But I cannot condemn, then or now, people who become alarmed and angry at their present plight. They are not Jeremiahs, because they express no opinions on the future, other than that they cannot see one for themselves. All they are saying is 'help'.

However, there is a further point to make in comparing the industrial revolution with the technological revolution. In the first case, we were innovators and pioneers and were thus able to reap the advantages that our head-start gave us over other nations. In this case, we are followers – not irredeemably behind the leaders, but far enough to give cause for concern. The Prime Minister recognises this better than anyone. In a speech at Brighton in 1981, she put it thus: 'There *is* a threat posed by the development of robots. And, in a way, it is a threat to employment; it is the threat of failure to compete: a failure which will face those who do not grasp the opportunities offered by robotics.' She was right. Failure to innovate will cause much worse economic, industrial and human problems than those I have described. But I think she misjudges the severity and duration of the problems that innovation itself will cause. A false view of the past is encouraging a false view of the future. What the Prime Minister says of the future is true, but it will take longer to realise than the Government supposes.

This approach adds up to government by hindsight and not by foresight. It applies hindsight to the first industrial revolution and anticipates the hindsight that history will apply to the technological revolution. It ignores the realities of both, as they are experienced by the people who live through them. If there is one passage in Kenneth Baker's speech that highlights this fact, it is this: 'In 1961, 8.4 million people had manufacturing jobs and 10.1 million service jobs. In 1983 the numbers in manufacturing had dropped by 3 million to 5.4 million and those in service industry jobs had risen by 3 million to 13.1 million.' This statement implies that there has been a straight swap of three million people between manufacturing and service employment. I would be more inclined to say the swap has been between manufacturing employment and the dole queue, with the three million new service jobs being filled through an increase in the number of working women and other expansions in the labour market. I would go on to say that this shows how difficult it is in human terms for someone who has previously held an unskilled or semi-skilled job in industry to make the unaided transition into either a service business or a new industry. We should not delude ourselves that any such thing is happening on a widespread scale.

While writing this book, I have noticed some signs of Government recognition of the problems suggested in this chapter. One or two Ministers have acknowledged that unemployment may well remain at three million or more for at least a decade. These admissions have been concealed in small paragraphs in the business pages of some papers. They have not hit the headlines and they do not amount to a formal Government statement, but they are a start. The test of the Government's intentions will be whether it faces up to this uncomfortable fact, or whether it continues to calculate that high unemployment will not prevent its maintenance of power, provided the rest of the nation is materially enriched.

In demonstrating the reality with which the Government must deal, perhaps it would help to set aside the intellectual argument and to consider the human reality. Imagine the rows of terraced houses in the old industrial cities, towns and communities of the North and the Midlands, all built around the sites of now decaying businesses and housing a large proportion of the unemployed and their families. Few of them are likely to work in manufacturing industry again. How are they going to turn themselves into an army of service industry employees? To whom will they be offering a service? Who can afford services in the vicinity? How are they going to move elsewhere? Where are they going to live? What jobs will they find elsewhere? How are they going to do it, physically, mentally or spiritually?

We are in danger of creating a large section of the population that is permanently unemployed, living in communities of terminal decay. Computers may brighten innumerable classrooms, but they do not prevent many children from regarding school as a waste of time, life as a meaningless prospect and delinquency as the only tolerable pastime. This is not the sort of future that we want, that they want, or that they need have. But that future will become the reality unless we take action now.

We must talk about these things. There is no need to be defensive about them. The Government is not to blame for causing the problems, nor is anybody else. There is no political stigma yet attached to the problems, nor any shame in admitting that ready answers to them do not yet exist. I freely admit that I do not have all the answers myself, but I do claim that I am asking the right questions. The opportunity is there. It exists for everybody. It will ultimately be fulfilled for everybody: the question is how long and difficult the period of transition will be. We need to make sure it is as short as possible, and involves the least hardship, disruption and alienation. To ask the Government to acknowledge this need is not an extravagant demand.

TEN

A Broad Party

'In every party there is someone who, by an over-devout expression of party principles, provokes the rest to defect.' – NIETZSCHE

Imagine a room containing Robert Peel, Benjamin Disraeli, Stanley Baldwin, Winston Churchill, Harold Macmillan and Margaret Thatcher and try to guess the consequences. Would Disraeli, Churchill and Macmillan stand in the middle, sharing a joke and a brandy? Would Peel and Thatcher engage in earnest conversation in a corner? Would Baldwin sit on the sofa quietly smoking a pipe? The possibilities are endless and diverting, including the chance of blazing arguments. Apart from the fact that all six have been Conservative Prime Ministers, it is hard to think of anything tangible they share in common. In different ways, they represent as great a diversity as the nation they have served.

Anyone who wishes to understand why the Conservative Party has survived for so long (it has some claim to be called the oldest political party in the world) and why it has formed the Government of this country for more than sixty of the last hundred years, might start by reflecting on the diversity of its leaders. This provides the key to the main strength of the party – its success in adapting to the needs of changing times. When one considers the degree of change over the last century, the scale of the achievement becomes even greater.

In this chapter, I want to consider the meaning and history of Conservatism, not as an academic exercise, but to give perspective to the party as it is today. Apart from the fact that such a study is interesting in its own right (at least to Conservatives), this book would be incomplete without it. I have a great respect for the tradition and spirit of Conservatism. Loyalty to that tradition and spirit has been and remains a principal purpose of my political life; I cannot imagine belonging to another party. The interpretation of that tradition and spirit informs each chapter of this book and all I have ever said or believed. The values of that tradition and spirit need constantly to be affirmed, and their history recalled, by all who share them. The exigencies of the present offer a permanent temptation to forget the past, and thus often to obscure the future. If a party fails to recall its roots and experience, it courts eventual oblivion. Just because the Conservative Party has been a major political force for generations, we have no right to assume its perpetuity. Nothing should be taken for granted. Our success in the future will depend on how well we reinterpret old values in a new world.

If the main strength of Conservatism is adaptability, its main enemy is ideology. By their nature, ideologies are inflexible, propounding what purport to be absolute and universal truths and demanding wholehearted adherence. The ideological blight of our age is doctrinaire Socialism and that is indeed its nature. One consequence of Socialism has been to encourage Conservatives to see themselves primarily as anti-Socialists. This can lead to a mistaken tendency to substitute one ideology for another. Conservatives have traditionally opposed ideology in every form. Long before Socialism entered British politics, the Conservative Party opposed the rigid principles of nineteenth century Liberalism, and for the same reasons: that they did not take account of people and they did not take account of circumstances.

Conservatives do not believe in a man-made Utopia, nor in a rainbow path that leads to a crock of gold. We do not start with the blueprint for an ideal world, but with an understanding of the real one and a desire to improve it however we can. We dislike ideologies both for their own sake and for their presumption to be the most important thing in life. We do not forget that most tyrants in history have shared this presumption. Conservatives do not believe that politics are the most important thing in life, let alone that they constitute life. We do not believe that any rigid doctrine is the answer to all the problems, because such a belief flies in the face of human nature, common sense, history and personal experience.

Instead, Conservatism is an approach that flows from life, not a doctrine to be imposed on life. It stems from an understanding of the wealth and diversity of life itself, its paradoxes and absurdities. It demands a sense of humour. It also demands a recognition that life only has meaning in terms of the individual, and that the greatest political vocation is to weld together the hopes, fears and feelings of millions of individuals into a harmonious nation. It is pragmatic rather than ideological. It does not lack ideals, but it prefers to base them on human values and not on intellectual principles.

This approach has important implications for how we perceive and handle change, how we view the concept of the nation and how we approach the role of Government.

Conservatives are not opposed to change. Indeed, we recognise that the only certain thing about life is that it does change. Certainly, we do not equate change with progress and we have always resisted both abnormal change and an abnormal pace of change. We ride the rhythm of natural change, neither forcing nor opposing it unduly. We have usually managed to avoid a tendency towards reaction on the one hand, or slavish addiction to fashion on the other. We recognise that the rate of change is not constant: that there are moments when great change is called for and others when the tide of life needs to move more slowly. Above all, we envisage change in terms of building brick by brick, and not of tearing everything down and starting again. For that reason, the protection and strengthening of institutions like the Monarchy, Parliament, the Law and the Civil Service have been a constant theme of Conservatism through the centuries. The aim has always been to conserve what is good and to improve what is bad.

Such an approach demands the sense of a unified nation. This is the most important element of true Conservatism. The things we most need in national life – stability, harmony, prosperity, a shared sense of purpose – can only be achieved through a diversity of people working together, learning to build on what they share in common and to tolerate their differences. An ideology accentuates differences. It may create a wonderful togetherness amongst those who share it, but it can create a bitter polarity between them and those who do not. It is the tragedy of every ideology to believe it can convert the whole world to its cause; ideologists can never understand the fact that most sensible people are always opposed, not just to their ideology, but to any ideology.

The Conservative approach must be national and not sectional, whether in terms of class, colour, ideas, wealth or anything else. Precisely because Conservatism is based on human values and an abiding temperament, it must seek and represent those values and that temperament wherever they are found in society, which is everywhere. Another unhappy consequence of the rise of Socialism, with its claim to represent working-class interests, is that it has encouraged the Conservative Party to be seen – and sometimes to see itself – as anti-working class and pro-middle class. This is a false view. The Conservative Party has always drawn support from the full spectrum of society, because it has usually sought to serve the full spectrum of society. Throughout the nineteenth and twentieth centuries, it has done as much if not more than any other party to improve social and working conditions and to create a better life for all the people of Britain. It pioneered the Factory Acts and much other social legislation in the last century that helped to mitigate the unacceptable face of Victorian values. In this century, it was co-author of the Welfare State and has instigated many other social reforms.

From all these attitudes stems the Conservative view of the role of Government. We have never assumed that the Government knows what is best for people and we have resisted the interfering encroachment of the State. However, just as important, true Conservatives have equally abhorred the laissez-faire attitude of nineteenth century Liberalism. We do not believe that the Government should step back and let people do everything for themselves, when it is obvious that many people will always need help and that the Government can often provide it. In this area, as in every other, we are not dogmatic. We have no fixed notion of the role of Government. We do not believe that Government intervention is always good or always bad. It depends on circumstances. If the Government can usefully intervene to improve life for people, it should do so, but it should never do more than it needs to do. If successive Conservative Governments had not taken this attitude, much of the legislation of which we are most justly proud would not have been enacted.

The Conservative approach requires a sensitivity towards change, a strong sense of national unity and a flexible view of the role of Government. I cannot claim that we have always been perfect in following these convictions. At times, we have lost touch with the nation and have broken step with circumstance. We have failed as human beings do fail. But we have been sufficiently true to our convictions enough of the time to have been the main party of government in Britain for most of the last 150 years.

Throughout this period, the Conservative Party has contained innumerable divergences, with different traditions and different factions arguing their own cause. That is one of the most healthy things about the party. The only way for Conservatives to heal differences in the nation is to contain those differences within its own ranks and to heal them there as well. If the Conservative Party ever became the repository of one point of view, it would cease to be the Conservative Party.

There are radicals and reactionaries: indeed, there are radical reactionaries, and quite a lot of them at present. There are authoritarians and libertarians. There are interventionists and disciples of laissez-faire. There are ideologues and pragmatists. There are traditional Tories and a wide assortment of Whigs, Liberal Unionists, National Liberals and others that have been absorbed over the years. In the erstwhile slogan of one of the more colourful Sunday newspapers, 'all human life is there' – and quite rightly so. Through the decades and the centuries, the conflicting views of these traditions have been exposed, argued and almost invariably reconciled.

The habitual use of the terms 'left-wing' and 'right-wing' is a great disservice to political understanding. Labels may be necessary, but they sometimes confuse more than they explain. These terms are certainly inadequate to define the differences in the Conservative Party. A single axis is insufficient to measure the subtle but important distinctions, and – more important – a straight-line axis is false to life, since it dictates that the left-wing extreme (Marxism) is as far away as possible from the right-wing extreme (Fascism), when both experience and common sense suggest that the two extremes are almost inseparable. A more apt visual image would be a heart, in which both extreme views meet at the bottom point, moderating gradually as they travel round their respective sides and finally pouring together into one point at the centre. Within the enclosed shape of the heart, all manner of subtle differences can be concealed.

The harmony of the Conservative Party has never been to do with a crude balance of right and left, but with the absorption of a wide range of views and attitudes. The party has survived because it has always managed to find a central harmony that binds the disparate elements together. It has achieved this by combining a strong motive for unity with a firm refusal to let ideology threaten it. The motive has been the desire to be a party of government. The Conservative Party has a strong instinct for power. Over time, it has acquired a habit of governing, in much the same way that the Liverpool football team has acquired a habit of winning. After a while, it becomes natural and gives a permanent competitive edge when other things are equal. Power is the incentive.

However, the mere desire for power is not enough to unite a party. The Labour Party has sought power with equal passion, but this has not served to unite it. The reason is that ideology precludes unity unless it is shared by all, which it never can be in a governing party. Ideological Socialists hunger for power. They sincerely believe that extreme Socialist policies should continue to be offered to the electorate as the best means of achieving it. How can they go on believing what everyone else in the country knows to be a complete fantasy? Very simply. All ideologists are convinced that their ideology is the answer to everything, so they invariably think it is only a matter of time and persuasion before everyone else accepts what has been obvious to them all along. Therefore they will not compromise, because compromise tarnishes 'The Truth' and prevents its universal acceptance. Therefore they will not listen, because everybody else is wrong. Therefore they can never be reconciled to people who disagree with them. Their answer to any criticism is to restate the ideology, deny the possibility of an alternative, shut their eyes to modification and, in the case of the Labour Party, drive their saner colleagues to defection.

The Conservative Party has seldom been ideological, although it has always contained ideological elements. Few of its members have believed that they possessed a monopoly on the truth, and those few have generally been wise enough not to say so. Dissenting views have been tolerated and heard. Seldom has anyone felt excluded from the workings of the party. In handling its differences, the party has usually been relaxed, tolerant and civilised. In this way, it has contained a broad spectrum of opinion and out of the mix has produced policies that, while they cannot please everyone, win the consent of all. That has been the genius of the Conservative Party. As I put it during a speech in the House of Commons immediately after the 1983 Election: 'At its best, the Conservative Party has always been broad in its view, national in its interest, tolerant in its outlook, constructive in its debate, and unifying in its aim'.

This approach is sometimes called 'consensus politics', usually in a pejorative sense and by people who presumably think that the highest form of political achievement is to get their own way at all costs. They are right. It is consensus politics. But let us be clear about what the phrase means. Consensus politics do not reflect the lowest common denominator of all viewpoints, and need not reflect the most prevalent viewpoint on any issue. They can sometimes apply to an unpopular or controversial course. The vital point is that the word 'consensus' relates only partially to the policy itself, but essentially to the means by which the policy is agreed and implemented. That is why the phrase is 'consensus *politics*' and not 'consensus *policies*'. By involving people in the process by which policy is developed, listening to what they say and adapting one's approach if necessary, one is likely to win consent for the policy itself – or at least far more consent than would otherwise be the case.

Consensus politics are the practical corollary of a concern for the whole nation. Governments that consider their entire purpose to be the enactment of party policy or of their particular ideology, ignore their first obligation, which is that they have been elected to be the Government of the country, the whole country and nothing but the country. Of course members of a Government should not abandon their own convictions and adopt compromise policies on principle. But neither should they regard elections as the beginning and end of the process of winning consent for what they wish to do. A concern to carry people with you is a permanent duty for a politician, even if protected by power from the practical need to do so. That is what is meant by consensus politics: listening to people, taking their legitimate views into account and carrying them with you as far as you reasonably can.

The Conservative Party has survived because it has practised consensus politics with great skill for many years. It has seldom become impaled on any single issue. It has never fought beyond the penultimate ditch. It has not been a refuge for martyrs to lost causes. It has always believed that the unity and continuity of the party are more important than any one issue or personality. The length of its life is commensurate with the breadth of its appeal, which is in turn commensurate with the latitude for differing views to exist. Good leaders have attracted unswerving loyalty to themselves by allowing individual members to remain loyal to their own convictions. They have served the party, rather than expecting the party to serve them. In that way, both unity and continuity have been assured.

One advantage of such a long history is the opportunity to learn from it. Empirical evidence is available to support what common sense suggests. Whenever the party has behaved in the way I have described, it has always been in power or close to it; every period of failure has been preceded by a deviation from its true nature. There are four episodes in Conservative history that I want to recall, because they illustrate four abiding concerns: the danger of party division, the importance of national unity, the difficulty of overt radicalism and the threat of ideology.

The danger of party division is best exemplified by the consequences of the one and only time in Conservative history when the party was comprehensively split. The cause was the determination of Sir Robert Peel to repeal the Corn Laws in 1846. Peel was a formidable politician and his achievements as Prime Minister, Home Secretary and party leader were immense. Furthermore, his motives in wishing to repeal the Corn Laws were admirable and the measure he proposed was necessary. However, there was little chance of his persuading a majority of the Conservative Party to support him, and the way in which he approached the issue exacerbated the problems. Convinced of his own rectitude, he was insensitive to the views of others. In his attempt to carry the measure, he displayed the subtlety of a sledgehammer. As a result, not only was the Conservative Party split from top to bottom, but it was nearly extinguished in the process and was unable to form a proper government for twenty-eight years, to the benefit of the Liberals, who would have passed the measure anyway.

If this episode shows the threat of dogmatic leadership to party unity, the 1930s provide evidence of the dangers of a divided nation. As it happens, I think Stanley Baldwin was a greater leader than most people acknowledge and it is my opinion that, in the circumstances of the Depression, he did as much to sustain national unity as he reasonably could. But, despite his efforts, the nation was deeply divided and the stigma of unemployment became attached to the Conservative Party. Those who argue, as many do, that such a claim is invalidated by Baldwin's resounding election victory in 1935, ignore two important facts. The first is that the Labour Party was in disarray in 1935 and quite incapable of providing an alternative Government. The second is that the ghosts of the 1930s were, to say the least, an important element in the 1945 Labour landslide and continued to haunt the Conservative Party for years to come. Political parties usually reap what they sow, even if the crop sometimes takes a long while to appear. It took many years and all the skill and enlightenment of men like Rab Butler and Harold Macmillan to erase the memory of the 1920s and 1930s in the popular mind, and to restore the reputation of the Conservatives as a 'one nation' party.

The third lesson of history concerns the problems that confront a Conservative Government of radical disposition. Conservatism and radicalism need not be incompatible, but they sensibly prefer to indulge in brief and passionate flirtations rather than a permanent relationship. The problem is that, while Conservative Governments frequently need to adopt radical measures and are often rewarded for doing so, they are seldom elected for that purpose. Two of the most radical Conservative leaders were Benjamin Disraeli and Harold Macmillan. The genius of both was to disguise the fact, or at least to make it palatable to the party and to the nation. Both pursued radical, liberal policies cloaked in the rhetoric of the centre and sometimes even of the right. You can call this cynical and deceptive if you like, but I would not. As I have argued elsewhere, intangible qualities like tone, style and approach are as much a part of the substance of politics as the policies themselves. Making change acceptable to people is directly relevant to every politician that ever lived. I therefore believe that, when Conservative Governments wish to be radical, whether from the 'right' or from the 'left', they are well advised to present themselves from the centre. This reduces the risk of divisiveness and improves the chances of successfully implementing reform.

The final lesson from the past is the danger to the Conservative Party of ideological obsession. In this context, I would like to examine in detail what happened in the early years of this century, when Joseph Chamberlain attempted to convert both the party and the country to a doctrinaire economic policy that became known as 'tariff reform'. This period of Conservative history tends to be ignored, perhaps because it brought such disasters in its wake. People forget the strange fact that the party, which had held power for seventeen out of the twenty years before 1906, winning three out of four elections, contrived to lose the next three elections and not to form a Government again until 1922. To blame Chamberlain and tariff reform exclusively for this fiasco would be an over-simplification, but he and his policy were the major reason for the failure. What drove the Conservative Party to such self-destruction?

The first point to make, and perhaps the real explanation, is that Joseph Chamberlain was not a Conservative. He would not have identified himself with the Conservative tradition I have described, and there was no reason to expect him to do so. Most of his political career was spent on the radical extreme of the Liberal Party, and it was only towards its close that he first adopted and then hijacked the Conservative Party. Until then, he had been a vitriolic scourge of Conservatism. He was a vigorous, self-made Midlands industrialist, who established his political reputation as a dynamic and reforming Mayor of Birmingham. In national politics, he combined laissez-faire economic dogmatism with a strong commitment to social reform.

It hardly seemed credible in the 1870s and early 1880s that such a man would end up in the Conservative Party. But, despite his other views, Chamberlain was a fervent nationalist and imperialist. His concept of nationalism was almost the antithesis of 'one nation' Conservatism: it was based on dogmatic attitudes both within the nation and internationally, rather than on the desire to seek reconciliation. It was divisive in its nature because it was one man's vision of nationhood, instead of the nation's view of it. As a result, Chamberlain was unable to stomach Gladstone's policy of Home Rule for Ireland. The Liberal Party split. Chamberlain led a break-away group of Liberal Unionists, which eventually allied with the Conservatives. Towards the end of his career, he actually joined the Conservative Party, and there his heirs and successors have remained.

Chamberlain possessed many personal and political qualities. He had great energy, determination and charisma. He was a politician of conviction, even if his beliefs differed from those held with equal conviction by others. He was passionate and persuasive. He was a practical man, who preferred to implement ideas rather than to debate them, and who was more concerned with power than with status. But he was also ideological and iconoclastic, neither of which traits sits easily with Conservatism. He may have been restrained in the pursuit of personal power, but he was ruthless in the pursuit of his ideas. Like most ideologues, he was a prisoner of those ideas and not their liberator.

Chamberlain never became leader of the party. His only chance to do so was in July 1902, when the Marquess of Salisbury retired. But, at that stage, he was the leader of the Liberal Unionists: he was not likely to be chosen to lead the Conservatives, nor did he expect or attempt to do so. Arthur Balfour, the heir apparent, duly became Prime Minister. But, from 1902 until illness forced his retirement in 1906, he can reasonably be said to have led Conservatism, even though he did not lead the party. It was at the beginning of this period that he embraced the policy of tariff reform.

No policy should be considered without its background. The background to tariff reform was the economic and imperial malaise of late-Victorian Britain. Despite the industrial and colonial achievements of the nineteenth century, a staleness had crept into the nation. Other countries were overhauling us economically, notably America and Germany. The British economy was in relative decline. At the same time, the imperial dream was turning sour. The Boer War of 1899–1902 was at times a military disaster and, in its effect, a psychological disaster. The future seemed uncertain: confidence was eroded and self-doubt prevailed.

Against this background, Chamberlain offered an approach that was new, radical and invigorating. He proposed the rebuilding of economic and political power through a regeneration of the imperial ideal. The policy was founded on the past, but it gave hope and purpose to the future. It sought to make the Empire a preferential trading partnership and to develop it into a united power bloc in the world. I know too little of the circumstances to assess the policy but, in this context, I am less concerned with the policy itself than with the political battle that surrounded it.

There were three attitudes to tariff reform within the Conservative Party in the early 1900s. A small number of traditional free-traders (about 60 MPs) opposed the policy on principle. A larger number (about 130 MPs), led by Chamberlain, were passionate advocates of the policy. The remainder (about 200 MPs), led by Balfour, agreed with the principle of tariff reform, but were concerned about some of its consequences and argued for a more flexible implementation. Although the policy was intended to benefit the whole country, Balfour felt it would be seen as an attempt to impoverish the working class.

Chamberlain refused to accept a dilution of the policy and continued to pursue it with ideological fervour. He even resigned from the Cabinet in 1903 so that he could more freely advocate tariff reform and challenge the prevailing fiscal orthodoxy. The immediate consequence was a public display of Government confusion. The party was divided, not so much between tariff reformers and non-reformers – as I have said, almost the whole party supported the intentions of the policy – but between the ideologists and the pragmatists. The events of 1904 foreshadowed later disasters. In that year, not only did tariff reformers fare disastrously at several by-elections, but Chamberlain's dogmatism drove Winston Churchill to leave the Conservative Party and to cross the floor of the House of Commons to join the Liberals.

These events seemed to double Chamberlain's determination rather than subdue it. The Conservative Party fought the 1906 election on the policy of tariff reform and suffered the most humiliating defeat in its entire history. At the previous election, the Conservatives had won 334 seats and a majority over the Liberals of 148. In the space of one Parliament, this was transformed into 156 seats, with a Liberal majority of 223. There were other reasons why the Conservative Party should have lost the

1906 Election, but the main cause of such a crushing defeat was the ideological insistence on tariff reform. In his book on '*The Conservative Party from Peel to Churchill*' (to which I am much indebted), Robert Blake states:

All the evidence suggests that nothing was more disastrous to his party than Joseph Chamberlain's campaign for tariff reform. The attack on free trade alienated Whitehall, for the whole weight of Treasury orthodoxy was against protection in any form. It alienated the economists – only four of any standing were in favour of it. Far more important it frightened a great section of the working class to whom cheap food had been a much cherished boon for the last quarter of a century and it annoyed the middle class rentiers who saw the prospect of a reduction in the purchasing power of their fixed incomes. It split the Conservative Party from top to bottom, creating a disastrous appearance of vacillation and dissension. Finally, it united the Liberals, who had been hitherto hopelessly divided on all the main political issues. This is quite an achievement for any campaign.

Chamberlain did not see matters in this light. He believed that the 1906 catastrophe demonstrated, not the unacceptability of tariff reform, but the need to pursue it with even greater fervour. He concluded that the key to success lay in strengthening the hold of the ideology within the party. Such a process was already well under way. Between 1903 and 1906, the Tariff Reform League had set out to capture constituency organisations at a grass-root level and had done so with great ruthlessness and success. By 1906, 300 constituency organisations were under its control, as was the National Union of Conservative Associations. But Chamberlain was still not satisfied. After the 1906 debacle, he demanded a meeting of all Conservative peers, MPs and candidates to agree a mandatory party line on tariff reform. Balfour tried to stall and was rescued only by the fact that Chamberlain suffered a severe stroke shortly afterwards. With his effective departure from politics, the ideologists lost their leader and the pragmatic centre was gradually able to reassert itself.

It is impossible to read the preceding paragraph and not to be struck by the remarkable similarity with events in the Labour Party over the last decade. One need only change a handful of names and dates for the description to be exact. In both cases, the same phrase was used to justify the process: 'party democracy'. In both cases, the intention of 'party democracy' was not to imbue the party with a more representative range of views, as its name might imply, but to secure the triumph of a single view. In both cases, the battle reflected, not a healthy argument over different policies, but the systematic attempt to impose an ideology on a party.

Chamberlain shared the assumptions of every ideologist: that his own doctrine was the unalloyed truth, that its purity must not be compromised, and that all other opinions were wrong and must be repelled. Like other ideologists, he would no doubt have been appalled at accusations of divisiveness. In his view, the self-evident truth of the policy meant that, once it was implemented, everyone would admire its wisdom. Why bother about winning consent in advance, when it would be forthcoming afterwards, as people came to realise how wrong they had been? In this way, Chamberlain came to equate loyalty to the Conservative Party and to the nation with loyalty to his particular ideology. Anyone who was disloyal to the ideology was immediately considered disloyal to the party, and was thought to lack any judgment of the national interest.

Chamberlain's illness in 1906 and his retirement from politics brought the immediate age of Conservative ideology to an end, but he bequeathed an impossible legacy. The party still believed in tariff reform, all the more so after his constituency manoeuvres, but increasingly realised that the policy was unacceptable to the nation. There was no ready cure for this dilemma: tariff reform could be neither painlessly abandoned nor successfully pursued, and the problem was not finally resolved until the 1930s. It is tragic that a man of Chamberlain's talent should have had such an effect on his adopted party. He was the most formidable politician of his time: a man of principle, a man of ideas, a man of action. His ideas were not necessarily wrong, nor were they incompatible with Conservatism. The problem was less with the policy than with the dogmatic insistence on its literal implementation, a disregard to its effects as perceived by the nation, a disinclination to listen to moderating influences, and a rhetoric that polarised opinion and exaggerated the differences instead of reconciling them.

The Chamberlain era confirms the danger to Conservatism of a betrayal of its true nature. Together with the earlier examples, it suggests that, while circumstances always change, the same issues repeat themselves over and over again, although in different guises and not always requiring the same response. Learning the lessons too rigidly can be as bad as not learning them at all, which is why the experience of appeasement in the 1930s led to such a calamity at Suez and was misapplied more recently over East–West relations. Each set of circumstances is in some way unique: history is a vital aid to contemporary judgment, but it should not replace the judgment.

It is the different circumstances of history, and the Conservative talent at adapting to them, that has produced such a wide diversity of party leaders. Yet they do share one thing in common. There was a moment when each of them appeared to be the right person in the right place at the right time. This is as it should be. In every walk of life, different people have different qualities, appropriate to different situations. Someone who is perfect for one job will be wrong for another, and just as wrong for the same job at a different time. The necessity is to keep the choice as wide as possible. Today's heresy is tomorrow's orthodoxy, which is why heretics should be kept within the ranks wherever possible. Anyone in the 1930s who saw Churchill as a future Prime Minister was regarded as a laughing-stock. It is even more unwise to be dogmatic about the future than it is to be dogmatic about the present. The person who best symbolises today's requirement may be least able to forecast tomorrow's requirement. The history of the Conservative Party is a permanent reminder of these truths. Always there is a need to keep the party broad, to keep the options wide, to listen to people, to draw them together, to win their consent, to make them feel wanted, to care for the whole nation and to care for the whole party.

This is the essence of Conservatism, although its nature makes it almost insusceptible to formal definition. Each leader has interpreted it in an individual way and has brought unique and personal qualities to the job, as well as a wide divergence of political opinions. Many leaders have departed from some of the principles; a few have departed from most of them; perhaps none have embodied them all. There is no sacred flame, handed down from one leader to the next, demanding scrupulous veneration and observance. But there is a core, both of thinking and approach, which most leaders have shared and which has served the party well throughout its history. Its success is due to the fact that, at most times, most people in Britain have themselves shared the same thinking and approach.

Today there is much talk about breaking the mould of British politics. The historic concern of the Conservative Party is not to break the mould, but to bind its contents together.

ELEVEN

The Politics of Consent

'The consent of the people is the only foundation of government.'
– JOHN ADAMS

The world of politics is a merry-go-round, in which we all ride our particular hobby-horses as they rise and fall in response to a mechanism we never quite perceive. The same horses gallop through history, eternally chasing each other's tails. Only the riders change. The fashion is to say that this cavalcade is important only to the riders, and not to the spectators or to the world at large. Politicians, it is said, over-estimate their influence on events. That is true, but a substantial influence remains and it matters to the nation how it is exercised. What is more, the broad questions and conflicts of politics mirror the questions and conflicts of life itself. Ultimately, we all ride the same merry-go-round. That is why an approach to politics can only evolve from an approach to life. In the end, the two are inseparable.

The previous ten chapters have ranged far and wide, covering many different subjects and contemporary issues. But the approach is constant and the same perspective has informed them all. Now, at the close of the book, I would like to draw its themes together. They can be summarised as individuality, interdependence, balance and understanding. These themes form the basis of my approach to life, and thus to politics. In this concluding chapter, I want to emphasise the values of each and to assert their relevance to political leadership.

How is one to view the battle of life? Is it a confrontation, a conflict of wills, in which annihilation of the enemy is the objective and his humiliation the trophy of war? Or is it a challenge to abandon our narrow trenches, to take the step into no man's land, and to meet the inhabitants of other trenches? Throughout history, people have given different answers to these questions. Often, no free decision has been available: the fact of conflict has provided its own answer. Today, we have the luxury of the choice, and I think it matters greatly how we use it.

I do not wish to view life as a battlefield, nor people who disagree with me as my enemies. In fact, it is because I see the easy attraction of this view, and its devastating outcome through the ages, that I am convinced of the need for the opposite view. The unrestrained exercise of individual will has produced the worst excesses of history, because it precludes relationship with others. The harmony of the world depends on its countless human relationships. A balanced individuality is the rock on which the most secure relationships are built. Rampant individualism is the rock on which they founder. That is why the two counterpoints to my convictions are Marxism and individualism. In running to their respective extremes, they produce the same effect. It makes little difference to the oppressed whether ideology or ego is the oppressor.

A respect for individuality demands the rejection of all forms of Marxism. During recent decades, Marxists have created a language trap into which many others have fallen. The trap is to present the world with the choice between Marxism and capitalism. It is true that such a choice exists, but it is not the complete choice, since neither system exists as an economic creed alone. The economic antithesis of Marxism is indeed capitalism. But the political antithesis is democracy. The spiritual antithesis is spirituality itself, and thus all forms of religion. The social antithesis is freedom. The moral antithesis is respect for the individual. Many people who dither over the choice between Marxism and capitalism would rapidly lose their doubts if they understood the real choice: Marxism versus capitalism, democracy, religion, freedom and the individual.

Marxism subjugates all expressions of individuality, wherever it can. That is why it will fail. It may yet enslave the world in its failure, but it will still fail. Individuality cannot be eradicated: not even the systematic brainwashing of humanity could accomplish that. The unit of the human world is the individual. It is only as individuals that we find our first meaning. Even collectivist theories spring from the ideas of individuals. Millions of people have lived on the earth over thousands of years, and no two of them have been identical or ever will be. Nothing so contradicts the essence of life as the imposition of uniformity. A state of independence is naturally ours: strait-jackets make prisoners of us all.

Therefore, unlike Marxists, I believe that life begins with the individual. But, unlike individualists, I do not believe it ends there. An approach that is over-weighted to individualism becomes one-sided. It breeds a world of steel, where people forge shields for defence and sharpen rapiers for attack, and parry all hints of sensibility. It pretends to a self-sufficiency that can never fully be realised. However strong and self-reliant any of us may be, we are all dependent on others. The long march of civilisation from barbarism to today has had many facets, but prominent amongst them has been the enlightenment to recognise that long term self-interest is incompatible with unrestrained self-will. Without that enlightenment, civilisation would have been impossible.

This recognition has developed over the centuries, enhanced by a greater understanding of our natural environment. Science confirms what instinct suggests. We can now appreciate that interdependence echoes through the far reaches of the earth, and touches every aspect of the human world. Life is a partnership. Each individual is dependent on other individuals for both material and emotional needs, whether we choose to acknowledge this or not. Within any nation, all members of society must see themselves as interdependent, or society cannot function. In the world at large, each nation is dependent on others for its peace, stability and prosperity. Interdependence is not an intellectual notion, imposed on life at one point in the world's history: it is a truth that stems from the heart of life itself. All living things are dependent on other living things. We are none of us self-sufficient.

Interdependence must be rooted in individuality, otherwise it becomes servitude. But equally, without a sense of interdependence, true individuality cannot exist. Rampant individualism contradicts itself. Its most vigorous champions are often least sensitive to the individuality of others. If individualism is not balanced by a respect for other people – that is to say *all* other people – and a tolerance of their views, it becomes oppressive. It confirms one of the many paradoxes of life: that most attitudes, if pushed to their extremes, devolve into their opposites. Extreme individualism is selfish, tyrannical and self-defeating. It tramples on most individuals so that a few can get their own way. It makes relationship with others almost impossible, whether on a personal level, within society at large, or between the nations of the world. If nothing else matters but oneself, nothing finally matters.

In this way, interdependence and individuality are not competing demands, but complementary aspects of life. Each makes the other stronger. The greatest strength comes from the best balance between them. Imbalance in either direction weakens the whole. It is like using the two tubes of Araldite – the adhesive and the hardener: the strongest bond is obtained by using precisely the same quantities of each. In life, individuality is the hardener and interdependence the adhesive.

The bonds of society are weakening at the moment and they may weaken more in the future. New technology offers us greater wealth, greater leisure and greater means to personal freedom, but – like most things that have the capacity for good – it also has the capacity for harm. If the benefits do not become available to everyone at a reasonably early stage, society will be divided and put under strain. If the benefits encourage the pursuit of individual acquisitiveness and diminish the sense of social responsibility, the strains will be equally severe. If the benefits are not met by greater self-discipline, and if the time we gain is squandered or abused, again there will be great strains.

The danger comes not only from selfishness, but from fear of communication. People already talk to each other less than they did, especially within families. A dependence on impersonal placebos is replacing a dependence on each other. We could yet become a nation of zombies, spending idle hours glued to television sets and video screens, absorbing an endless jumble of information, understanding less and less, and failing to communicate with each other at all.

At the moment, there are embryonic signs of these dangers within our society. I do not want to overstate them, and I do not predict they will have the consequences I have described. But they are all there: the gap between the new industrial élite and the old industrial discards, an increase in selfish individualism, an absence of self-discipline, a decline in communal values, a refusal to take the consequences of freely-made decisions, reduced personal communication, greater boredom and greater tensions both within society and within individuals. If these signs are recognised, there is no need for them to take effect: only if they are ignored will the danger materialise.

Perhaps more than anything else, we need to develop a new moral framework for society. Until recently, the absence of self-discipline was disguised by the strength of exterior disciplines, and especially by the need to work long hours to satisfy material needs. Those exterior disciplines have crumbled and, unless we develop the self-discipline to replace them, our freedom will turn into anarchy. Nothing has yet replaced the work ethic and the other moral concepts of a world we are now leaving behind. The new framework must somehow encompass how we can use greater leisure and greater freedom for constructive self-expression and for relating to other people and to the world around us, and not for the destruction of social and human values. Self-discipline and social consideration must be its cornerstones. And that is why my theme of a balance between individuality and interdependence is more urgent and relevant now than ever before.

That balance is required throughout society, and it needs to be reflected in politics. There is too little balance in political life at the moment. Two opposed extremes do not create harmony, just as two wrongs do not make a right. At best, they cancel each other out. The excesses of the hard left are well-known, but the attitudes of the new right are not much more palatable. Together, they create a world of black and white. Everything has to be cut and dried. False polarities abound. One set of extremes is extolled; the other is assailed. But the true contempt of both sides is reserved for everything between the two extremes. It is significant how many intellectuals of the new right used to be doctrinaire Socialists. They delude themselves that they now believe the opposite of what they once believed. But the light on their own particular road to Damascus is a mirage. To swap one extreme for another is a small change compared with forswearing all extremes and seeking the balance in-between. That would be the true conversion.

There is no refuge from the weight of history. More than two

thousand years ago, the cult of extreme opinions was the subject
of this denunciation by Thucydides:

> To fit in with events, words too had to change their usual
> meanings. What used to be described as a thoughtless act of
> aggression was now regarded as the courage one would expect
> to find in a party member. To think of the future and wait was
> merely another way of saying one was a coward. Any idea of
> moderation was just an attempt to disguise one's unmanly
> character. Ability to understand a question from all sides meant
> that one was unfitted for action. Fanatical enthusiasm was the
> mark of the real man. Anyone who held violent opinions could
> always be trusted, and anyone who objected to them became a
> suspect.

The evangelists of the hard left and the new right give contemporary meaning to this warning, and it frightens me. Once the
balance is upset, the consequences of imbalance become pervasive and unpredictable. Destructive forces are released. Politics
begin to jar with nature. The diversity of life is no longer
honoured, but threatened with extinction.

Balance is not the soft expediency that extremists offer as a
caricature. It is tougher to find the means to unite people than to
give expression to what divides them. Nothing is easier than to
spout violent opinions that glory in their disregard of others. Nor
does balance imply uniformity. We are all individuals and we will
always have our independent opinions. But somehow those
opinions have to be reconciled if civilised society is to exist.
Extremists can never reconcile differences: they start by accen-
tuating them and end by trying to suppress them. Politicians
cannot afford to do either. If we want to reconcile differences, we
have to listen to people and try to understand them. Not just some
people. Everybody. We have to accept that people who do not
share our own values or opinions are not inferior, and may not
even be wrong. The slanging match of politics is eternal, but there
is always a need to look behind the rhetoric and to consider what
reasonable people think is reasonable.

Just as there is a need to understand people, there is a need to
understand circumstances. Conservatives must understand why

Labour Governments are elected and vice versa. No one can force their will on the world if the times are against them. Life has its own rhythm and resents opposition. We know that in our own lives it can suddenly become easy to do things we have struggled to do for ages, and the same is true in politics. The tide turns. Where once it has been impossible for a Government to implement reform, it becomes almost impossible for it not to do so. More political change has been brought about by the tide of events than by individual will. If one fails to appreciate the role of the tide in political success, it will eventually engulf one in political failure. Politicians who do not understand this tide are no wiser than King Canute's courtiers.

An understanding of time and tide demands an understanding of paradox. Decline begins at the zenith of success. Each ending is a new beginning. The greatest strength lies in restraint. Taking other people's views into account makes acceptance of one's own views easier. Extreme attitudes engender their opposites, as do extreme policies.

Such an understanding breeds tolerance and a sense of humour. It precludes dogma, ideology and absolutism. When a single beam is mistaken for the sun, all other rays are extinguished. The same sun shines on everyone, but it shines through many windows and strikes us daily in a different light. If a set of temporal values is enshrined as a creed, it cannot remain relevant for long. What is most in fashion at one moment will be most out of fashion the next. Nothing absolute is right for every occasion.

By purporting to deal with all times, dogma never truly confronts any. Its blinkered vision sees the past in the light of the dogma's absence, the present in the light of its application, and the future in the light of its assumed triumph. In this way, it misunderstands the past, has only a partial view of the present and fails to anticipate the future. Dogma is a painting without perspective. Dogmatists cannot come to grips with the world, because they cannot come to grips with themselves. Inflexible opinions defend against inner doubt, not outer adversaries.

A respect for individuality, a belief in interdependence, a search for balance and an attempt at understanding amount to one approach to life, and become one approach to politics. Such an approach can be shared by people of widely different political opinions: the only opinion it precludes is the belief that only one opinion is the answer. It is therefore not to do with policies, but with the style in which policies are debated and put into practice. Qualities like courage, determination and toughness can belong to this approach as they can belong to any other, although they will manifest themselves in a different way. The approach is based on ideals, but it is also practical, and in a sense rather selfish: it asserts that one is more likely to get one's own way if one does not try too hard to do so. In politics, it seeks the best of both worlds: to make what one wants to do acceptable to other people.

That does not mean it is a sham. People see through shams. The approach will only work if it is honestly pursued and leads to action that seeks to benefit the whole nation. When people say they do not trust politicians, they may be expressing a healthy scepticism about our moral virtue, but they are also reflecting the fear that we do not have their interests at heart. In other words, they believe that many politicians only listen to one section of the community and only govern for one section of the community.

Trust is built not just through the honesty with which intentions are stated, but through the honesty and fairness of the intentions themselves. Confidence is built not just through the assertion of present policy, but through the consideration of future needs. Strength and determination are qualities of leadership, but they do not amount to leadership. The great leaders, both in war and in peace, have of course been strong and determined, but they have always shown a concern for everyone in their care and they have always tried to anticipate the future.

This approach amounts to my definition of political leadership. It requires a broad and impartial role for a Prime Minister as the head of a united team, the arbiter between a range of views, and not as the main protagonist on every issue. When there are two teams and the Prime Minister plays centre forward for one of them while trying to act as referee, the Government cannot be balanced, since to side with the other team is to oppose the referee. Such a role also makes perspective difficult. One cannot detect the flow of the game if one is always embroiled in the tackle.

The preceding pages are the philosophical justification for the politics of consent. The experience of the centuries is their practical justification. The approach does not guarantee success:

like everything else, it depends on how it is operated and in what circumstances. But, over time, this approach has usually advanced human progress, while the politics of confrontation have usually retarded it.

The politics of consent are neither a luxury nor a soft option. They are the only form of democratic politics that will ultimately work or that can have a moral basis. Government is based on the rule of law; law is based on justice; justice must be based on a rough consensus of definition. If one does not listen to people, one will fail to perceive the consensus. Attempts to change the consensus need to be gradual: healthy societies, like friendships, build on themselves. One cannot knock the consensus down through brute force and start again. Society no longer coheres through brute force, but only through the consent of its members. Governments must earn this consent and earn it constantly. Elections are the formal means by which consent to a Government is granted or withheld, but they do not obviate the need for consent at all points in-between. Such consent can only be achieved if expressions of dissent are heard. When Governments view all contrary opinions as obstacles to be overcome and silenced, they are on the way to tyranny.

Life cannot operate without consent from the smallest scale of human relationship to the largest. No family can survive if its members pursue their individual wills to the exclusion of others. Nor can any community. Nor can any nation. Nor can any group of nations. Nor can the world at large. The scale is different, but the principles are identical. One must listen to people, try to understand their point of view, try to accommodate their wishes and try to win their consent. In short, one must be considerate to others. This may be an unoriginal approach, but it happens to be true to my nature and, in my opinion, it conforms to the instincts of at least half the world. It is an approach to which mankind will always return when the tedious touting of extremes loses its glamour.

During the course of this book, and especially in this chapter, I have mentioned what I see as the related failings of dogma, ideology, imbalance, individualism and insensitivity. People will wonder to what extent such comments are intended as direct criticisms of the Government in general and of the Prime Minister in particular. I would rather answer that question myself than

encourage speculation and possible misinterpretation. What I am
attacking are extremes and, when I have attacked the attributes
above, I have attacked them as extremes. In that sense, they are
aimed generally and not specifically. I do not believe the Government or Prime Minister to be extreme, and to say they were would
be to fall victim myself to extremism.

However, I do think that these attributes exist as tendencies
within the Government and, if I did not feel this was both
important and worrying, I would not have troubled to describe the
dangers that could flow from such tendencies. Rightly or wrongly,
I believe they account for most of the Government's immediate
problems. The desire for the literal achievement of its plans is
leading both to undue haste and to an unhealthy degree of
centralisation. The style needs to become more balanced, more
relaxed. It may seem a facetious point, but much of the fun has
gone out of politics in the last few years, and I think it would help
everyone if it came back again. Fun and enjoyment do not detract
from the handling of serious problems. On the contrary, they help
us all to face them.

There is therefore some unease within the Conservative Party
at the moment. Most of it may lie below the surface, but the same
is true of the iceberg that sank the Titanic. It is not enough to
rearrange the deckchairs and to ask the band to play more loudly.
It is time to start noticing that people are looking for the lifeboats.
The unease concerns many things, but above all it concerns
political style and perspective. It is less to do with policy objectives
than with strategy and approach. It is not to do with who leads the
party, but with how the party is led.

The balance of politics is the balance of a see-saw. The degree
and direction of the tilt depends on the bulk and positioning of the
riders. There are times when a heavy weight at one end is needed
to counteract a heavy weight at the other. But neither end of the
see-saw can remain forever on the ground, since nature abhors
imbalance as she abhors a vacuum. Once the previous imbalance
is corrected, the bulk will start to shift towards the other end if the
positioning remains unaltered. Only by edging slowly towards the
pivot can the advantage be maintained. Nature will achieve her
balance one way or the other. In my view, the enduring balance of
the centre outweighs the restless motion of alternate extremes.